D0294999

Celtic Tales

Retold by
Elena Chmelová

Forevord by
Frank Delaney

TIGER BOOKS INTERNATIONAL

Designed and produced by Aventinum Publishers, Prague,
Czech Republic
Text by Elena Chmelová
Translated by Stephen Finn
Foreword by Frank Delaney
Illustrated by Zdenka Krejčová
Graphic design by Ivan Urbánek

Copyright © 1990 AVENTINUM NAKLADATELSTVÍ, s.r.o.

This edition published in 1998 by
Tiger Books International PLC, Twickenham, UK

All rights reserved. No part of this publication may be reproduced
or transmitted, in any form or by any means,
electronic, mechanical, photocopying, recording or otherwise,
without the prior permission in writing from
the publisher and the copyright owner.

ISBN 1-84056-026-6
Printed in the Czech Republic by Polygrafia, a.s., Prague
1/01/41/51-02

CONTENTS

FOREWORD

A story, say the wise, should have a beginning, a middle and an end. Something — or many things — must happen, caused by somebody, and with a reason. Stories may also teach — good and interesting things, or magic and odd things, or funny and crazy things. But the best stories of all are those where you, the readers, are left guessing, all the way through and at the end, as to whether or not the tale is true.

This collection of Celtic Tales satisfies all of those requirements. The Celts, who established one of the major early civilizations, came out of Central Europe. If you visit Austria today you can still see the graves where chieftains were buried along with their favourite possessions — dice, drinking cups, brooches.

The Celts were a fierce and warlike people who went into battle naked and painted in gaudy colours, striking terror into the hearts of their enemies with their wild shouts. But they were also a loving and imaginative people who sang songs, recited poems and told stories of their past. Today there are still people of Celtic origin in Ireland, Scotland, Wales and Brittany. They have their languages and their music and their timeless history, much of which was never written down, but came down through the centuries via the storytellers.

So, when you read in these pages about the King of Ireland who had twelve sons and, "not even the king, nor his queen, could tell which of them was the wisest, the best, the cleverest", or Yann, the Breton miller's son who rescued the seven cows from the cave of the dragon, or King Maxim who had to roam Wales for seven years before he married the Queen of Rome, who knows which is history and which is story?

FRANK DELANEY

INTRODUCTION

High above the waves, where the broad plains plunged headlong towards the sea, a little stone cottage nestled in a cleft among the rocks. In that cottage lived an old fisherman. His hair was like snow, but his hands were still strong. The years had curved his back, but he could still cast a net or bend an oar as well as the young fishermen. And none of them could match his knowledge and experience of the sea and the wide world.

From autumn to spring, the moment supper was over, people would gather around his hearth to hear him tell stories of the past. One night, when they were all seated, the youngest of the fishermen said, "Now then, Sean, tell us about the old days."

"Is it you as would be hearing about the old days, young Dan?" replied Sean's neighbour, a bent old man. "When you are the very one to go looking for something new? Why, tomorrow you are leaving for far-off places, and who knows when a fair wind will blow you back to us. It would be all very well if you were to take ship and sail for maybe a couple of days, just so that you might see what goes on by the shores of the nearest land — there's none of us has sat by his own fireside all his life. But you must be off to the other side of the world! Among strangers! There you will forget all the bold Irishmen who have lived here since time began."

"But it is not so!" Sean the Storyteller interrupted. "This has not always been the land of bold, red-headed Irishmen. The legends of old tell of how we came here from far away. Long, long ago our grandfathers' grandfathers lived, together with other great families, in tribes which spread like the branches of a huge tree through a fertile land. That was in the middle of old Europe, close to the upper reaches of two great rivers, the Danube and the Rhine. They were surrounded by hills and mountains which were overgrown with thick forests full of birds and animals. Through the valleys flowed rivers as clear as rain, and there were so many fish in them that the water would sometimes seem to boil as they swam upstream. Only the sea, our own broad sea, was far away, and none of our forebears even knew what it was, for they had never heard tell of so much water. But sea or no sea, they had plenty to eat and drink. There was nothing they liked better than to roast a lamb on the spit and to wash it down with mead."

"If only they had known how well off they were!" cried an old man who was sitting on the end of the bench. "I suppose they bathed in wine and dressed in silk!"

"Fine young lads watched over great flocks; they tilled fertile soil, caught fish in the rivers, smelted golden metal, and turned copper and tin into bronze. Craftsmen worked metals into beautiful bracelets and necklaces, and also into helms and shields, war-axes and hammers, swords and other weapons from which their enemies fled. They also made spearheads, with which the hunters killed many animals."

"Why did they ever leave that land?" asked Sean's neighbour bitterly. "Could it be that good living turned their heads? As for me, I should never be found in this wretched country of famine and want, if I had not grown up here, and if my great-grandfather's great-grandfather had not come here."

"As time passed, there were more and more mouths to feed," Sean went on. "And the more of them there were, the less game they brought home from the forests, and fish from the rivers. The fields no longer yielded grain enough for all, and in time only the old folk could even remember the good old days."

For a while Sean fell silent; then he continued: "As if all that were not enough, the country was invaded by warlike peoples from the north; they burned down the houses, robbed the stores of grain and weapons, and drove away whole herds of cattle and horses. By the time the warriors had pushed the enemy back, there was famine everywhere.

"For a long time the chief elder of the tribes listened to the lamentations of his people, until at last he called a council, which was joined by his three sons. He addressed the council: 'I am old; I have seen much and in my lifetime I have received much good counsel. But no one has ever heard of such misfortune as that which afflicts us now. Therefore I summoned the wise old men, to hear what they had to say. They all spoke with one voice, saying that there are too many of us, that the land cannot support us all. You then, my eldest son, shall gather together the strongest of the men, together with their families, and go in search of a new homeland. You, my second son, shall take those of the young men who are most skilled in smelting and metalwork, along with those who know most about horse-breeding. You shall live by those skills. And you, my youngest son, shall stay here with me, and rule over the tribes in my stead, when you have learnt all those things which a good ruler must know.'

"It seemed to many that they had never heard such dreadful words in all their lives. All night long old and young talked together; at sunrise, their deliberations had still not come to an end. All of them were anxious to know who was to leave his land and his home, and who was to stay. In the end they came to an agreement; they divided up the stores of weapons, grain, dried meat, hides and furs, wool, even the horses, and most of them set off in different directions, north and south, east and west. For a long time the wandering tribes sought new lands. They passed over many a mountain range, crossed many rivers. The great families drifted apart as if blown by the winds; then, as time went by, they came together again as if they had agreed where they should meet. Many of them died on the way, and many a child was born in a foreign land. And somewhere in Greece our forefathers got their name. The people there called them Celts, and the name was passed down from generation to generation. I do not know myself what it meant — some say warriors, other say something like mulish, stubborn folk. More than once my old father recalled how those nomadic Celts of long ago not only settled in many different places, but also knew how to defend their new homes. Once upon a time their enemies shook with fear as those valiant Celtic warriors fell upon them like a flood tide, their war cries mingling with the sound of trumpets and horns, the rattle of spears, the clang of shields, the ring of swords and the whistle of battle-axes. There was no escape from them. And when those warriors were seized with the excitement of victory, their campfires turned night into day."

Sean half closed his eyes, bent over, rested both his hands on the bench as if overcome with tiredness.

But Pat the blacksmith, a huge fellow, and the best singer for miles around, began to drum quietly with his fingers, and it sounded as if he were forging nails. "Don't you forget," he reminded Sean, "that in the furnaces of our forefathers the fires of peace burned day and night. No one feared those — they only looked on with envy as the iron came to life in their hands. They say that our forebears brought a rare metal, which people called iron, from somewhere far to the south, and that they learned to work the metal, to cut and chop with it, even to plough their fields with it."

"How could I forget!" replied Sean, with a quiet smile. "Nor have I forgotten how they admired great singers like yourself."

"And storytellers like you, Sean," grunted the blacksmith.

"Yes," said Sean. "He who composed songs and poems had a place alongside kings, dukes and earls just as a master smith did. So honoured were they, that they were given the best of food on golden plates, and kings toasted them from golden goblets. Pat, if only you had been alive then! The minstrels sang many songs, merry and sad, of beautiful women and brave men; but they also sang of the day-to-day life of our forebears, who laid the foundations of the renowned city of Dublin, and were the first to build in the places where London and Paris were later to stand. It was their hands which built a whole chain of cities and fortresses, which stand to this day in far-off lands. I think the sun itself would be hard put to it to look into every corner where our ancestors ever lived."

"Ay," agreed Pat the blacksmith, who had himself sailed the wide ocean more than once as a young man. "Our forefathers not only crossed mountains and rivers, but in the end they ruled the waves of the northern and southern seas. Their horses reached the banks of the Black Sea to the east, and one day their riders came to the place where the sun sinks into the western sea on the very edge of the earth, here in Ireland."

The guests smiled contentedly at having at last got to where they should be, and old Sean continued, "Here in the west at least a handful of the descendants of the ancient Celts remained, and they say that something beautiful and powerful has been passed on to them, something that will never die. The old songs, legends and tales are a bridge between the ancient times and now."

And that was all Sean the Storyteller was going to say for that night. The fire in the hearth had slowly burnt away, and the last embers had died. The visitors went their separate ways, amid the growing din of the sea and the wind, to come back again the next day, and hear again of the things that had happened long, long ago.

King Conal's Horses

Long ago there lived in Ireland a king whose wife had a heart of gold. She was loved by all the people, and smiled on rich and poor alike. If any pauper should come as a suppliant to the palace gates, he could always count on the queen's protection.

The queen brought three healthy sons into the world, and when they grew into fine young lads there was no happier family in the whole of the kingdom.

But one day the queen fell sick, and no one could find a remedy for her illness. When she realized that her last hour was at hand, she sent for the king and begged him to promise that he would fulfil her dying wish.

"Tell me what you would have me do, and I shall do all in my power to carry out your wish."

"When I am dead," begged the queen, "and after some time you marry again, promise that you will send our sons to some distant corner of the realm. I do not want them to take orders from any strange woman. Let them return to the palace as grown men."

The king gave the dying woman his word, and before long the queen had quietly breathed her last.

The king went into mourning for a whole three years, and refused to listen to the advice of his counsellors that a kingdom without a queen is like an orphan. But in the end he decided to take their counsel, and had a castle built for his three sons, far away from the royal palace. There he sent them, along with the best tutors and the most faithful of the servants. Then he remarried, and lived happily with his new wife. After a year the queen gave birth to a son, and once more the walls of the royal chambers rang with the laughter and crying of a baby.

One day the king went hunting, and the queen decided to take a walk outside the palace walls. As she was walking among the houses, she slipped on some steps and fell.

"Would that worse befall you!" called out an old woman from one of the houses.

"Why do you curse me, when I have never harmed you?" asked the queen, taken aback.

"Nor have you ever helped anyone," replied the old woman, gruffly. "The king's first wife was indeed different. If she saw that a pauper was cold, she would take the shawl from her own shoulders and wrap it around a poor old woman such as myself. She would not even sit down to eat, until she saw that all at her court had food enough. You, you care only for yourself and your son. But just you wait until the king's elder sons are grown up: then things will be different at the palace!"

The old woman's words filled the young queen with anxiety. She began to ask about the dead queen and her sons, but in vain. The old woman would say no more. But her tongue was loosed when the queen offered her a hundred sheep. Then she told her where the young princes were, and why they lived so far from the royal palace. The young queen only listened, and listened, becoming more and more afraid for the fate of her own son.

"I should give a hundred cows and a hundred goats to anyone who could tell me what to do to make sure that my son shall not be fated to wander without a roof over his head, like some poor bird in the air."

"If you will indeed give me a hundred cows and a hundred goats, as well as the hundred sheep you have promised, then I will advise you well."

The queen gladly promised all this, and the wicked old woman whispered to her, "Listen carefully to my words. You must persuade the king to invite his sons to the palace for a few days at least. By and by you shall ask them to play chess with you. I shall give you a chessboard with which you will always win. When you have defeated them all, tell them that you will set them a forfeit. Tell them to go at once to King Conal and take three stallions from his stables; say that they are to bring them here, for you wish to ride around the kingdom on them three times. The young men will go out into the world, and will never return, for many bold men have sought King Conal's horses, but none has ever been seen again. Then the future of your son will be assured."

The queen was well pleased with the old woman's advice, and when the king returned from his hunting she treated him with great affection, and asked about his sons. He told her why he had kept them a secret from her.

"Invite them home," the queen implored him, "so that I may at least come to know them. You will see how I shall love them as my own."

The king did as she asked; he sent a message to his three elder sons to come and visit him, to pay their respects to the new queen, and to greet their youngest brother.

Before long three riders, the young princes, were dismounting at their father's court, and the king at once gave orders for a great feast to be held in their honour. All were truly glad to see the princes again, and the young queen put on a great show of welcoming them the most sincerely of all.

After the feast the king had a great hunting party prepared, followed by an archery contest. The sound of singing was heard at court, and the young princes excelled in valour and skill. Day by day they became dearer to their father's heart, and he was overjoyed to have all his sons at home again.

Then, one day, the queen invited them to play chess with her. She produced the chessboard she had received from the old woman, and played against each of the princes in turn. She played three games with each, winning two of them and, for appearances' sake, losing the third.

That evening when the queen had played the last game with the youngest of the princes, the eldest asked her, "What forfeit will you give us, since you have defeated us twice?"

"All three shall have the same forfeit: promise that you will not sleep twice more beneath this roof, nor eat twice more at this table, until you have brought three of King Conal's horses. I should like to ride three times around the kingdom on them."

"Very well, o queen," said the eldest prince, with a bow. "Only tell us where we may find King Conal's horses."

"The world has four corners," replied the queen. "If you go to all of them, you are sure to find them."

"And now I shall set you a forfeit for the one game which I won," said the eldest brother. "You shall go to the highest tower of the castle and watch for us until we return with the horses."

The queen grew as pale as death.

"And I shall set you a forfeit for the game you lost to me," said the middle brother. "Until we return, you shall never once eat enough to satisfy your hunger, nor drink enough to quench your thirst."

"Take that back," begged the queen, "and I shall take back your forfeit."

"If a young man is freed of the first task he ever receives, then he will never come to anything," said the youngest prince. "Let us go in search of King Conal's horses."

Early the next morning the brothers took leave of their father and set out to find King Conal's castle. For a long time they wandered the world, and no one was able to tell them where they should turn their steps. Then, one day, in a solitary city, they came across a lame man in a black cap.

"Who are you, young fellows?" he asked them, when they greeted him. "And what has brought you to a city more frequented by beast than by man?"

"We are the sons of the King of Ireland," replied the eldest prince, "and we are seeking the castle of King Conal. Our step-mother has sent us for three of his horses."

"Many brave young men have sought the horses of King Conal, and none has returned alive. But perhaps fortune will smile on you. Come, you shall spend the night under my roof, and in the morning I will take you where you wish to go. Without me your travels would be in vain."

The three brothers thanked him kindly, and went to spend the night in the stranger's home.

The next morning their host woke them up, gave them a good breakfast and, setting his black cap on his head, led them on their way. Before evening fell, they had reached King Conal's castle.

"Now you should rest," the man in the black cap told them. "I shall wake you before midnight."

At midnight they crept stealthily into the stables. The guards were asleep, so it was without trouble that they reached the horses, took hold of their bridles, and began to lead them from the stables. But the moment they felt the touch of a strange hand, the horses snorted, stamped and neighed until they woke up the whole castle. The sentries jumped up, grabbed the four thieves, and led them straight to King Conal.

The king was sitting on a tall golden throne in a huge chamber, surrounded by guards with drawn swords. A fire was burning in the hearth, and over it hung a large cauldron.

"Guards!" called out King Conal, when they brought him the four horse-thieves. "Put more wood on the fire, that the oil may start to boil. And you, tell me who you are. If I did not know that the Black Brigand is dead, I should think you were he," he said, turning to the man in the black cap.

"I am indeed the Black Brigand. As you can see, I am alive, and I might almost say well."

"Hm," said the king, doubtfully, "you will not stay that way long. And who might you be?" he growled at the young men.

"We are the sons of the King of Ireland," replied the eldest.

"Well, I never!" cried King Conal. "Are even the sons of the King of Ireland horse-thieves? Very well, we shall start with the youngest." Then he turned to the Black Brigand. "You have seen many men close to death; tell me, have you ever seen anyone whose death was more assured than this young man's?"

"Indeed I have, King Conal. I myself was threatened by a death even more certain than that which awaits the youngest prince, and yet I stand here today."

"Very well, you shall tell me about it. If what you say is true, I shall spare his life."

The Black Brigand took a seat on the bench by the hearth, gazed into the flames, and told King Conal his story.

THE THREE ENCHANTED PRINCESSES

"Once I had plenty of land, cows, horses, sheep, and all I could wish for. I lived honestly and well, until three witches stole everything I owned. Since I had lost everything, I took up the robber's trade, until I became the most famous robber in the whole of Ireland. There was no one throughout the whole land who had not heard of the Black Brigand.

And the three witches who stole all my property were the daugh-

ters of the Irish king. During the day they were the most beautiful maidens in the whole world, but at night-time a powerful wizard would turn them into three ugly hags.

Before I lost everything, I once sent my servants to dig peat, and I told them to bring enough for seven years. They brought a great amount, and piled up so much of it behind the house that it looked as if a black hill had grown up there. Soon it seemed to me that this peat was being used up very fast, though I had no idea how that might be. But one night after midnight, as I was returning from some great celebration, what should I see? Three great ugly hags were stealing peat from behind the house. They loaded it into baskets, and then carried them away as easily as if they were quite empty. After that I lay in wait for them, but I was never able to catch them. All that winter they stole my peat, and by the time spring came my seven-year supply was all gone.

In autumn I had a store of peat for seven years brought once more, but again those three witches stole it all from me. But this time I was luckier, and one night I caught them as they were filling their baskets. They ran off up into the mountains with them, and I set off after them and saw them disappear into an underground passage among the rocks. I looked inside, and saw a huge fire burning there; on the fire was an enormous cauldron, and in the cauldron a whole ox was cooking. The three ugly hags were dancing around the fire. I looked around for something to throw at them. By the entrance to the cave I spied a large boulder. I pushed a branch from a tree under it, leaned on the end of the branch, and sent the boulder crashing down with a terrible din. It smashed the witches' cauldron, and the soup spilled out and put out the fire.

When I saw what had happened, I ran for my life, but before long the witches caught up with me. I could already feel their hot breath on the back of my neck, and they were almost treading on my heels. At the last moment I climbed up a tall tree, but even in the dark the hags spotted me there. They stood beneath the tree, glaring at me. They did not feel like climbing up, but the oldest of the three swiftly turned the middle one into an axe and the youngest into a savage dog. The oldest of the witches swung the axe and chopped away at the tree with all her strength. The dog leapt about beneath the tree, baring its teeth and barking fiercely. The first blow of the axe sank a third of the way into the trunk. The witch took another swing, and the axe bit two thirds the way into the trunk. The witch raised the axe a third time, and the tree would surely have come toppling down, had not a cock crowed at that very moment. Suddenly the axe changed before my eyes into a beautiful maiden, the witch who was chopping down the tree into another, and the dog into a third. Three beautiful maidens, the like of whom has never been seen in the whole of Ireland, nor ever will be. The sisters joined hands and walked away from the tree. They seemed to me as happy and as innocent as babes in their mother's arms."

"Now, tell me, King Conal," the Black Brigand asked the frowning king, "was I not closer to death at that instant than is the youngest of the Irish princes now?"

"You are right: you were indeed," admitted King Conal. "And therefore from this moment the youngest prince is my guest. But now it is the turn of the middle brother, and the oil in the cauldron is already on the boil."

"Indeed, but I have been faced with a death more certain than that which awaits the middle brother now, and I am here to tell the tale."

"Very well; we shall hear that one, too. If what you say is true, then I shall spare the second prince's life."

THE THIRTEEN TOMCATS

"The witches were not going to forget the trick I had played on them. From that night on they did not cease to harm me in every way they could. They killed my horses, throttled my sheep, drowned my cows in the bog. They stole my chickens, trampled my crops and burned down my barn. Before long I was faced with poverty. If

I wanted to keep my wife and children as befits a worthy man, I had no choice but to take to robbery.

At first I was not too successful, always making off with some sickly cow or half-blind horse. But when I managed to get my hands on both a cow and a horse at the same time, I was the happiest fellow in the world. I knew at least that my wife and children would not go hungry. But I was counting my chickens before they were hatched, and I was in for a nasty surprise.

I was driving the cow and the horse home that night, for robbery is night work, when I suddenly became so tired that I could no longer put one foot in front of the other. Since I was just passing through a thick forest, I tied the horse to a tree and the cow to another, and curled up myself beneath a third. I was cold, so I lit myself a fire and warmed myself in front of it. Before I got properly warm, I spied the thirteen biggest tomcats that ever were seen creeping up to me from out of the forest. Twelve of them were the size of sturdy young men, and the thirteenth was twice as big. That one came and sat down by my fire without so much as a by-your-leave, and then the others joined him. Six on one side, six on the other. The tomcats sat and warmed themselves, and their eyes sparkled and shone like great green fires. One after the other they began to purr quietly with contentment, and when they were all purring at once, it was like the rolling of thunder.

In a while the biggest of the cats raised his head, looked at me, and mewed, 'I am hungry; but I do not intend to go hungry any longer. Give me something to eat!'

'I have nothing to give you, except for that old grey horse, tied to yonder tree.'

The tomcats jumped up from the fire, mewed, and disappeared. In a while all thirteen of them returned, licking their lips, and sat down by the fireside once more. Soon they were purring away like a thunderstorm.

Before I could get round to thinking how I might give the tomcats the slip, the huge one spoke up again.

'I am still hungry; but I do not intend to go hungry any longer. Give me something to eat!'

[20]

'I have nothing to give you, unless it be that old cow which is tied to a tree over there.'

The tomcats leapt up, mewed, and were gone. But I knew well enough that it was high time I saved at least my own sweet life. I slipped off my tunic, wound it round a tree-stump, and stuck my cap on top, so that it might seem to the tomcats that I had fallen asleep by the fireside. Then I quickly shinned up the tallest tree I could find.

Soon the tomcats came back to the fireside, licked their lips, and began to purr like thunder.

In a while the huge ginger-tom again began to mew, 'I am hungry; give me something to eat!'

When there was no reply, he pounced on the tree-stump, sank his teeth into my tunic, and tore off my cap with his claws.

'Aha, so he has escaped us! But don't worry, my friend, we shall find you, even if you are flying among the clouds, or buried in the ground,' he growled.

Straight away he sent six of the cats to search the length and breadth of Ireland. The other six were to search beneath the ground. In the meantime the huge one sat beneath the tree.

Before long all the cats returned, saying they could find no trace of me. The ginger-tom rolled his eyes in anger, and at that moment he spotted me up in the tree.

'Aha! Now I have you!' he shrieked, and he ordered all the cats to gnaw through the trunk of the tree.

It didn't take those twelve tomcats very long to deal with the massive tree. They gnawed their way through the trunk, and the tree toppled at the feet of their huge leader. But as it fell, I just managed to grab hold of the branches of the one next to it. The tomcats set to work on that one, too, but at the last moment I leapt onto another tree again. Before long the cats had felled all the trees in that dense forest except for one, and I was in it. Now, I had no idea how I was to escape when my last refuge came tumbling down. That last tree was already keeling over, when suddenly, out of nowhere, thirteen wolves came running up. Twelve big grey wolves running in a pack, with a thirteenth, an enormous one, at their head.

The wolves pounced on the tomcats, and a fierce struggle broke out, such as I have never seen, before or since. They tore, scratched and bit at each other, until soon there were twelve dead wolves and twelve dead tomcats lying beneath the tree. Now the fight was on between the huge ginger-tom and the enormous wolf. On and on they fought, until at last both fell down dead. It was only then that I dared climb slowly down the tree, which was no easy matter, for its trunk was so gnawed away that it leaned over terribly and swayed from side to side. More dead than alive, I reached the ground at last, then ran home as if both tomcats and wolves were at my heels."

"Now, tell me, King Conal," said the Black Brigand, turning to the throne, "tell me truly: was I not closer to death than this Irish prince?"

"You were indeed, and from this moment the second son shall also be my guest. But the oil in the cauldron is boiling for the eldest."

"Let it boil, for an even surer death has awaited me, and yet I am here to tell of it," replied the Black Brigand.

"Then tell us of it, and if what you say is true, then the third prince also shall have his life spared."

THE UNGRATEFUL APPRENTICE

"When I had been at the robber's trade a year or two, I got to know it better than most. For robbery is indeed a trade, like any other. When I had mastered it, I took on a couple of apprentices to help me out. Among them was one lad who was especially skilful. I paid most attention of all to him, for he had sharp wits and deft fingers, and he went about his work with great zeal. Before too long I had taught him everything I knew, and more than once it seemed to me that he was more adept at the trade than I, for he was faster, more agile, and more cunning.

I had heard tell of how, on the other side of our land, there lived beneath the ground a giant who was rich beyond belief. His home was in a rocky cave, and it was filled with gold, silver and precious stones, for the giant would rob the richest lords in the land. So my apprentice and I decided we should set out to find this giant, wait until he was away from home, enter his cave, and take away as much of his treasure as we could carry. Then we should live like lords! We spent a long time searching for the giant's underground hideout, but in the end we found it. The only entrance to the cave was down a deep rocky chimney.

We watched the giant for several days, and discovered that he left his cave every morning and went off somewhere, returning in the evening with a large sack on his back. We supposed it to be full of gold, silver and precious stones.

One morning, as soon as we saw that the giant was well out of the way, I tied a rope around the apprentice and let him down into the cave. But before he was half way down the chimney he began to shout and pull at the rope, telling me to haul him back up again.

'I started to feel dizzy,' he told me. 'You go down, master, and I shall haul you up again as soon as you have collected enough of the treasure.'

So he let me down the chimney, and I found myself standing in a huge cave. Looking about me, I saw piles of gold, silver and precious stones winking at me from every corner. Opening my sack, I filled it with just enough of these riches for one good strong fellow to carry, tied it to the rope, and called to my apprentice: 'Haul away, but take care!'

I watched as he slowly and carefully pulled the sack upwards, and went off to fill another one with treasure. When it was full of the sparkling stuff, I called out to my apprentice to let down the rope. At first there was no reply, but then he called out, 'Thank you, master; my apprenticeship is over. I have nothing more to learn from you, so fare you well — and I hope your meeting with the giant will be an interesting one!'

For a moment I thought he was only playing a foolish joke on me.
But when he neither spoke again, nor let down the rope, I knew

I was probably in the finest mess I had ever been in. Only a fly could have climbed the smooth wall of the giant's rocky chimney. Quickly, I looked around for a place to hide, but I could see none that seemed safe enough. Then, suddenly, I heard a rumbling and crashing: I knew it could only be the giant. There was nothing for it but for me to fling myself down on a pile of dead bodies that lay in one corner. The giant was just climbing down with another three victims. He dropped them on the floor, and came over to where I was lying. He tore the clothes and shoes off the bodies, and stripped them of all their valuables. He took my clothes as well, and then threw me into a huge basket. After that he piled some more of the bodies on top of me, and carried the basket off to the back of the cave, where it ended in a deep abyss. I was right at the bottom of the basket, and managed to take a firm grip of the wickerwork. The giant tipped the contents of the basket into the abyss, and then, without looking inside, laid it in a corner upside down.

For a long time I listened to the giant's steps, then I heard a loud slurping, which told me he was having his supper. Then there was silence for a while, broken at last by the sound of heavy snoring. The giant was asleep.

'Now is my chance,' I said to myself, and crept quietly out from under the basket. I held my breath and tiptoed along the huge cave as quietly as only a robber knows how. I was looking around for some ladder or rope which the giant used to get in and out of the cave. I was in luck: standing against the wall was an enormous ladder, hewn out of stone. Whenever the giant left his cave, he would throw it down so that no one except another huge fellow such as himself might use it. But now it was ready to use, and I ran up it like a squirrel."

"Now tell me truly, King Conal: was I or was I not in greater danger of death than the eldest of the princes now?"

"You were indeed, and therefore the third of the Irish princes shall also be my guest. But do not suppose that the oil in the cauldron is boiling for nothing. You have had your share of close shaves, but you can scarcely have been faced with more certain death than you are now."

"Death is certain," replied the Black Brigand, "but its hour is uncertain. I tell you that I have been closer to it than I am now, and yet here I stand before you."

"Very well, then tell us about it. If it is true, then your life, too, shall be spared, and I will entertain you all grandly."

The Black Brigand shifted slightly on the stone bench, took his eyes off King Conal, and turned them again towards the leaping flames of the fire. The king and the three brothers listened in silence.

THE THREE GIANTS

"One day, on my travels, I was weary fit to drop and shivering with cold, and my stomach was aching with hunger. Then I spotted a house nearby. I went towards it. 'Maybe I can warm myself a little,' I thought to myself. 'If I am lucky, then perhaps they will let me sit at the table as well as by the fireside.' When I got to the house I found only a young woman with a child on her knee. The baby was smiling and chuckling, but the woman was weeping inconsolably.

'Why are you crying, instead of playing with the child?' I asked, surprised at what I saw.

'How can I laugh and play with the child, when we are both of us doomed to die?' she wailed, more desperately than ever. 'And if they find you here you are sure to meet the same fate.'

By and by, I managed to calm her down enough for her to explain to me what terrible house I had stumbled across.

'Last autumn I went to the fair in town with my parents. All of a sudden three huge giants descended on us; everyone was terribly scared, and in the turmoil the giants robbed them of all their valuables. Then the oldest of the giants caught sight of me, picked me up and threw me across his shoulders; after that he and his brothers made off with their spoils from the fair. They brought me here, and since then I have had to cook, wash and clean the house for them. But worst of all is that the oldest of them wants me to marry him. I begged him to wait a while, until I was eighteen, but in a couple of days it will be my birthday; truly, I should rather die along with this child, than have to be the wife of a horrible giant.'

'And whose is the child?'

'Yesterday the giants carried him off from the royal palace, and ordered me to kill him, so that they might be revenged on the king. They say that when the king finds he has lost his only son, and doesn't even know what has happened to him, he will search the whole world over for him. Then he will forget about the giants, and will no longer have them hunted. And if in the end folk do get to know that they stole him, then everyone will be more afraid of them than ever, and they will be left in peace.'

Now I knew all I needed to know.

'Do not cry, and do not be afraid; instead, you must listen to what I tell you,' I said. 'There is time enough for looking death in the face: let us rather think of a way of escaping her. Here in this sack I have a pig. Put it on the spit and roast it as fast as you can. Then get ready plenty of ale and whiskey. I shall hide in the cellar with the prince, and see what can be done to save all three of us.'

When the giants returned, I took the little prince in my arms and hurried off to the cellar. There were enormous casks there, and huge pieces of meat hanging from nails. I hid with the child in the darkest corner, where I hoped to wait until the giants fell fast asleep from their feasting.

But not a bit of it: how were the giants to fall asleep, when the roast pig failed to satisfy their hunger? First of all the youngest of them came down to the cellar. He was unsteady on his feet, and he leaned on the cask behind which I was hiding, as he tried to cut off a piece of meat that he wanted to roast. As soon as he turned his back on me, I drove my knife into it, and the giant crashed to the floor. Before long the second of the giants came down after his brother; he was looking around for the best piece of meat, when he stumbled over the first giant's body. I stabbed him, too, and left him stretched out across his dead brother. Truly, I do not know how long it took, but sooner or later the oldest of the giants came into the cellar, too. He found his brothers, and when he picked them up he saw that they were dead. Searching about furiously, he soon found me hiding there. He hurled himself upon me, swinging a huge club about his head; he brought it down with such force that it made a hole knee-deep in the ground. But I managed to jump out of the way, and the club did me no harm. While the giant was pulling his club out of the ground, I rushed up to him and stabbed him three times. He must have had nine lives, for he still had the strength to get in one more mighty blow with his club. Though he missed me, I was gravely injured when the club sank deep into the stone of the floor, sending splinters of granite flying in all directions. Then the giant fell dead on top of his brothers, but I collapsed not far away, blood pouring from a wound in my side. I thought my eyes were closing forever, when I heard the girl beside me.

'Now I can die happy,' I said, 'since you are both saved.'

'There is no need for you to die,' she said. 'Hold on a little longer. The giants have the water of life: I shall take you to it, and the wound will be healed.'

She managed to lift me onto her back, and took me to a neighbouring cellar, where there was a great cask, filled to the brim with water. But that was the last thing I saw. As the girl leaned over the water of life with me, the light was extinguished from my eyes, and I fell into a swoon. Had I not leaned over the water of life, I should surely have died. But the healing water brought me to my senses, and soon gave me back my strength, so that I was able to leave the cellar on my own two feet."

"Now tell me truly, King Conal, was I not closer to death then than I am now?"

"You were indeed," assented the king. "And even had you not been, you would from this moment on be the dearest guest in the whole world to me. For had it not been for you, I should not be sitting here today. I am the lad you saved from the giants that day. My father told me I was rescued by the Black Brigand, and he searched high and low for you, but never found you. Then I myself tried to find you, but I gave up when I heard a false rumour that you were dead. I am truly happy to be able to welcome you in my palace."

Before long the servants had prepared such a banquet in the royal hall as has seldom been seen, or even heard of. Then King Conal showered the Black Brigand with gifts; he was generous towards the princes, too, and he agreed to lend them three of his horses.

"When you no longer need them, you have only to turn them loose," he told them. "They will return of their own accord."

The three brothers thanked both King Conal and the Black Brigand, and took the shortest route back to their stepmother. From the tallest tower, she saw them while they were still far off.

"Have you brought me King Conal's horses?" she called.

"We have brought them, as you ordered," replied the eldest prince.

"I shall come down at once!" she cried.

"Wait a moment," replied the middle brother. "We did not promise to give you King Conal's horses, for that was not what you required of us. You only asked that we should bring them, and we have done so." With these words the brothers turned the horses loose. The three stallions neighed loudly, threw back their manes, turned, and were gone. The thunder of their hooves grew fainter and fainter.

"Still, I may come down from the tower, and eat and drink my fill," said the queen. "For have you not returned?"

"Indeed we have returned." It was the youngest brother who spoke now. "But stay in the tower: you forget that I have still to set you a forfeit for the game you lost to me."

"Then what do you ask of me?" said the queen, stamping her foot angrily.

"Only that you remain in the tower until you find another three royal princes to go in search of King Conal's horses."

When the queen heard this, she threw herself from the tower in despair and ended her wicked life.

How Gwion Became the Most Renowned of All the Singers

Once upon a time, long, long ago, a certain mighty lord had a pretty young wife and two children. His daughter was the loveliest and most charming little girl you could imagine. You only had to see her golden hair and eyes like a clear blue sky, and at once you forgot all your troubles. The lord and his lady would have been happy and

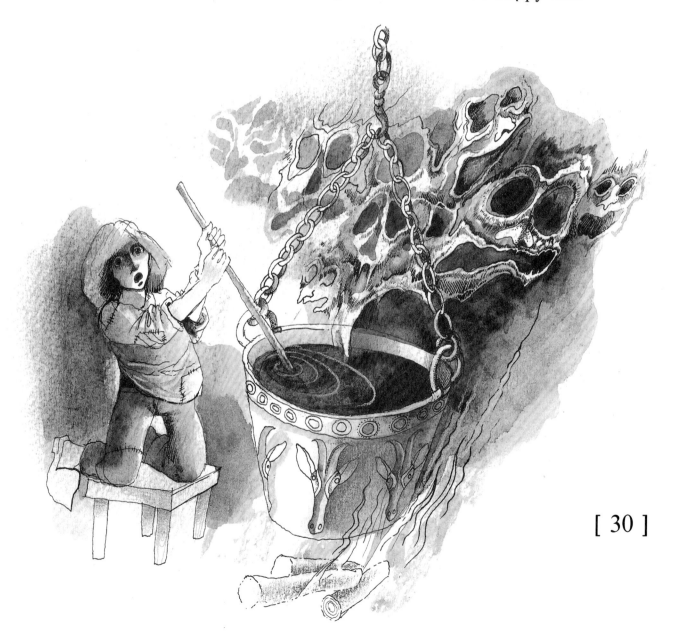

contented, had not their son been the ugliest lad for miles around. He had hair like a clump of hay, eyes like a thundercloud, and pocked cheeks, so that there was many a scarecrow made a prettier sight than that young man.

The lady grieved terribly; she would hide herself away in some corner and secretly weep, and whenever she looked at her son, the smile would freeze on her lips. But all was to no avail — the lad grew uglier day by day. In the end his mother resolved that if her son was the ugliest lad for many a long mile, at least he should be the wisest in the whole world. Then perhaps his looks would not matter so much.

From that moment on she left no stone unturned, visiting one wizard after another, and going from wise old woman to herbalist, to ask how her son might grow up to be the wisest man in the whole world.

On the advice of magicians and sorcerers, she hung a large pot over the fire, poured into it all kinds of waters known to have magic powers, and added a host of different herbs, so that in a year and a day she might brew up a potion which would give her son untold wisdom. Every month she added more spices and herbs, according to the recipes she received. Little by little, the lady got to know the magic art.

From the moment she began to weave her own magic spells, the servants were forbidden to go near the cauldron, so that no one might see what she put in the potion, nor overhear the magic words she spoke over it. She found an orphaned boy from the village to skim the brew with a great golden ladle, to stir it, and to tend to the fire, so that the embers beneath the cauldron glowed day and night, like the eyes of a pack of ravenous wolves.

"Gwion," the lady promised the boy, "remember that I shall reward you well if you serve me faithfully for a year. You shall have new clothes; there will always be food on the table for you, and when your task is completed I will give you a purse full of coppers to take with you. But mind that not a single drop is spilt from the cauldron, or it shall be the worse for you!" The boy was overcome with fear, until he began to shake all over, so his mistress soothed him: "Have no fear; I see that you are a clever lad. You need only take care."

In a while the boy himself did not know how long he had been mixing the brew, day and night, skimming the froth from it, and mending the fire. From time to time his mistress came and sat beside the cauldron, sending the lad off to sleep. Almost a year had passed, when, early one morning, the pot started to boil a little too vigorously, the froth came up, and three drops of liquid as black as pitch splashed on the lad's hand. Gwion swiftly licked them up, stirred the brew, and skimmed off the froth, before he might get into trouble. All of a sudden he heard a whispering sound from beneath the window. It was the trees, whispering in the wind, and Gwion could understand what they were saying. He could understand the little birds in their nests, too; they were whining that they were hungry. The lad was so pleased with his good fortune that it was a wonder he didn't leap to the ceiling with delight; but he knew well enough that he must not give away so much as an inkling of how much wisdom he had acquired from the three drops.

At dawn the mistress came to see if the brew was boiling and the fire burning beneath the cauldron. There were only three more days to go before the year and a day was up, and she could hardly wait. As she looked at Gwion, the lad read the truth in her eyes, and he saw something he had never dreamed of! His mistress was not going to give him a suit of clothes, or a purse full of money. As soon as the potion for her son was ready, and she had strained it off into a golden goblet, she was going to reward the boy for his faithful service by seeing to it that he disappeared from the face of the earth. She was afraid he might reveal the secret of how her son had come upon so much wisdom. But she in turn saw the truth in Gwion's eyes. She knew at once that the lad had tasted the magic liquor. It would have been the end of him, had he not thought at that moment that he would like to be a hare. Before the idea had properly crossed his mind, he was leaping through the open door, long ears and whiskers flattened by wind; he dashed across the courtyard, leapt over the wall, and disappeared into the undergrowth beyond the deep moat.

His mistress, too, wasted no time. By means of a powerful spell [32]

she turned herself into a greyhound, and in three huge leaps she was in the bushes. The boy froze with terror when he saw the dog, but he managed to say quietly, "I want to be a fish in the water!" — and right away a silver trout was hiding beneath the thick roots of an old willow tree. The witch changed into an otter, and plunged into the water beside the willow. As she peered around in the water, she heard the sound of wings above her head, and looked up to see a little bird climbing towards the clouds. In a flash a hawk was hovering over the poor little creature, its great wings blotting out the sky. The little bird changed into a grain of barley, and fell straight into the chaff on the barn floor. A large black hen was hunting around there for a grain of barley, pecking here and there with her sharp beak. Now she found one, and pecked it in two. One half fell from her beak, and changed back into human form. But since half the grain was gone, Gwion, too, was smaller than before, and the witch found a little baby lying there in the straw. She quickly changed back into a pretty young woman, unhooked a basket from a nail, and carried the baby off in it, down to the sea. She threw the basket into the water; the waves rocked it gently, then the current carried it away, straight towards the cliffs.

The lady returned home, pleased with her work. But when she reached the cauldron, she froze with horror. The black liquor had boiled away while she was chasing Gwion, and the herbs had burnt to the bottom of the pot. All her trouble had been in vain; now neither spells nor weeping and wailing were able to help her.

It so happened that Prince Elphin himself was just rowing into the bay to see if his nets had filled with fish during the night, and he spotted the basket twisting among the eddies between the rocks. He caught it with a hook, lifted the lid, and was greatly moved by the beauty of the child he saw inside. Quickly, he took it in his arms, wrapped it in his own woollen shirt, and rowed for the shore as fast as he could, to save the little foundling. The women at his castle fed the child and looked after him well, and day by day the boy grew in beauty, strength and wisdom.

On the very day of the lad's seventh birthday, the prince was attacked while out hunting by a band of men belonging to the northern king, and taken as a prisoner to the royal castle. In the prince's castle both old and young wept and wailed, but all to no avail; no one knew how to set the prince free from his cruel prison.

In the end little Gwion spoke up: "Give me a horse and an escort, and I shall go and set the prince free."

But the princess only smiled sadly. "What can you do, my child, when all our captains and soldiers are powerless before the might of the king's castle?"

"But I shall not set might against might," the lad replied, boldly. "I shall throw them into such confusion that they will not know whether they are standing on their heads or their heels, and in the end they will set the prince free whether they like it or not."

For good or ill, in the end the princess gave in to the boy's pleas, and prepared him for his perilous journey.

"And now we shall race the wind!" called Gwion, as they turned northwards. When they were all ready to fall off their horses with weariness, he urged them on: "Time enough to rest when our prince is at liberty. Remember that he is in chains, shivering with cold and tried by hunger. It would be shameful for us to rest."

At long last they arrived, exhausted, beneath the walls of the royal castle. The guards grinned disparagingly when they caught sight of that tattered band of horsemen, led by a boy. But Gwion threw back his head and called from afar:

"Open the gates and announce us to the king! I have come to confound your sages with riddles, and to out-sing your miserable minstrels. Have a place prepared for us at the king's table!"

The counsellors and singers, lords and servants all shook their heads in disbelief to hear such words from a slip of a lad. The king himself only laughed. But when they told him the boy's cloak was embroidered with gold and his saddle set with precious stones, like a prince's son, he ordered a place to be made ready at the table for the unknown company.

"My lord," began Gwion, after they had supped well, "I have come to outwit your wisest counsellors, and to sing in place of your best singers, for I have heard that your minstrels sing like young cockerels learning to crow."

The king reddened with anger, and motioned to his singers to sing his favourite song, of the mightiest of all castles and of his kingdom above all kingdoms. But the boy fixed his gaze on the singers, and by a magic spell made them sing and play out of tune; they made a terrible row, and it really was like cockerels learning to crow.

"Enough!" roared the king, beside himself with rage. "Now you!" And he pointed to Gwion.

"Very well, my lord," said Gwion. "But first allow me to set your four-and-twenty wise counsellors such a riddle that they will not solve it before daybreak!"

Now not only the king, but all the courtiers too were seized with anger.

"If my counsellors indeed fail to guess your riddle, then you may ask of me what you will: I shall fulfil your every wish!" cried the king. "But there shall be two sides to the bargain: if they solve your riddle, neither you nor your company shall leave here, so that you may learn that those who make fun of the king and his counsellors do not escape just punishment."

"Believe me, my lord, I should never make so bold as to poke fun at you. But if I do win the contest, I would ask you to grant me one wish."

The whole of the royal court was amazed at such boldness. The wisest men in the whole of Wales were gathered in the royal hall, and now here was some young whippersnapper who thought he would make fools of them in front of the king himself. They began to whisper among themselves that the lad should be sent packing from the royal court. But Gwion slowly surveyed the assembled counsellors, and then spoke thus:

"Tell me, sirs, what is it that is the mightiest of the mighty, for the fields and forests bow to him; he has no body or bones, no head or arms and legs, and he flies the length and breadth of the earth, though no man has ever seen him!"

The sages took counsel; they guessed this and that, not only till daybreak, but a whole three days and nights without sleeping. Still, they were unable to solve the riddle.

"We give up!" the oldest of the counsellors said at last.

[36]

"If you did not spend all your time peering into dusty books and sitting at table in the halls of kings and princes, then you would know at once that it is the wind," smiled Gwion contentedly.

The courtiers were even more enraged than before that such a stripling should have fooled them for three days and three nights, and they wanted to get rid of Gwion. It occurred to no one to ask him what he required for having won the battle of wits. But suddenly a quiet murmur was heard in the distance. It grew steadily louder, until it became a rumble, then a roar. A strong wind got up, then a storm broke, which turned into a full-blooded tempest.

The savage wind tore the roof from the tower in which the king had imprisoned his captive, and lifted him in the air like a feather; the chains fell from his limbs as if they had been sawn through. Prince Elphin was as free as a bird. Then the wind came rushing into the royal hall, and before the courtiers knew it, they were carried right up to the ceiling. The king, his counsellors and all the rest of the court were hurled about among the servants and guards, as if they were all dancing in the air. They were unable to stay still for even a moment, or to touch the ground, until, one by one, they solemnly swore to leave Elphin and Gwion alone, and never more to persecute them, or their children, or their children's children. Only then were they set free, at Gwion's command. All of them landed back in their places in the hall, and the singers and their instruments got back their voices.

No wonder the fame of Gwion's wisdom spread quickly throughout the whole kingdom. By and by there was no more famous singer in the whole of Wales; when Gwion began to sing, the rest were silent. His voice drove away loneliness, and brought the whole world to life; his words were like a powerful spell, which made everyone forget time. To this day, therefore, the name of Gwion has not been forgotten.

The Silver Hare

Once upon a time, long, long ago, a mighty Breton lord lived by the sea. His wife died young, leaving him an only son and three pretty daughters. In time, when the sadness and grief of his loss had passed, the lord might have lived in happiness and contentment, had not three giants suddenly made their home in a nearby forest. Who knows where they came from, but they were so fearsome that all the inhabitants shook with terror at the very mention of them. And not for nothing: they stole whatever they could lay their hands on, driving into the forest cows, horses, sheep, goats, loaded carts, and more than once even people. The lord could think of no other way to pro-

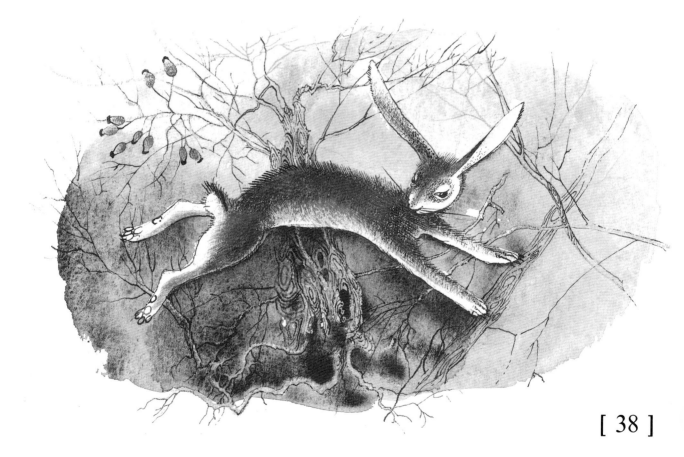

tect his mansion than to have a huge stone wall built around it, and to place guards all over the garden.

The three daughters were forbidden to leave the fortified mansion, in case the giants should do them some harm; they were only allowed to take a little walk every day. The son would go into the forest to hunt from time to time, accompanied by a well-armed escort. It was indeed a dull and joyless life, filled only with fear and anxiety. Things were bad, and they were soon to get worse. One day, as the young man was returning from hunting, he was greeted at the mansion by loud wailing and lamentation.

"Alas, my son," groaned his father, "your eldest sister has suddenly disappeared, before her sisters' very eyes, as they were walking in the garden. It was as if the ground had swallowed her up. The giants have surely carried her off by some trick or other."

It was a wonder the lord's heart did not break, and he at once gave orders to double the guard throughout the house and gardens. But it was no good: the next month the middle sister stepped out into the courtyard, and suddenly disappeared from view like her sister before her.

The mighty Breton lord grew weaker day by day, and wasted away with grief. The youngest daughter did not so much as set foot on the mansion steps; she did not stir from her chamber, and even there she was guarded at every step. But all the same, before another month was out, the sound of weeping and wailing was heard again throughout the house. The girl had disappeared from her chamber during the night, as if some evil wind had carried her away.

The unfortunate lord died of grief, and his son Malo did not set foot outside the house for many a long day, but only mourned his father and his sisters. By and by, as he became oppressed with loneliness, he went out hunting, to drive away a little of his sadness. He walked, and walked, pushing his way through the thicket, but he did not see a single animal or bird in the whole forest. Then suddenly he spotted a hare whose coat shone like silver.

"A pity to shoot such a fine-looking hare," he said to himself. "I should rather catch him and let him go in the gardens." As if he understood that the hunter did not wish to shoot him, the hare stood and looked at him boldly, without so much as twitching an ear. Malo was just about to raise his hand to throw his net over the hare, when the animal came to life, leapt up and ran off a little way. Then he sat down again, as if waiting for something.

The hare played this game with the young hunter for a long time. In the end Malo grew angry, took his rifle from his shoulder, and shot at the creature. But the hare did not bat an eyelid, and the bullets did not so much as scratch him.

"What sorcery is this?" cried the young man, angrily. "Truly you have magic powers, if bullets do not harm you; who knows where you are leading me to?"

"I shall tell you where I am leading you," replied the hare, in a human voice. "I am taking you to your eldest sister. On the other side of the thicket you will find a mansion; in it lives your sister."

At that instant Malo was too excited to be surprised that a hare was talking to him; he forgot all about the hare and all about his hunting, and ran off to find his sister. He found himself standing before an old mansion surrounded by a high wall. When he banged on the gate, he heard the voice of his dear sister from up above him.

"Who is it?"

"Your brother Malo. At last I have found you, my sister!"

His sister was beside herself with joy, and quickly ran to open the gate. She embraced her brother, hugged him tight, and then sighed, "Dear brother, I am afraid for you. In a while my husband will return, and he may harm you. He is not wicked, but he is a ferocious giant. He eats six roast oxen at one sitting, and I can truly never tell what he will do next . . ."

Malo was taken aback, but he did not allow his sister to see it.

"I don't suppose he will eat me," he laughed, "Hide me somewhere, and in the morning I shall move on."

The eldest sister hid her brother in the corner, behind a row of large barrels. At that moment the giant opened the gate and came in, leading six oxen. He called out from afar:

"Wife, I have brought our supper!"

He sat down at the table, and it was a wonder the bench of rough oak trunks did not snap beneath the weight.

"I am tired; give me some wine," he growled.

The young woman took a silver bucket, filled it with wine, and stood it in front of her husband. He took a deep draught, but suddenly cried, "Ugh! The wine is tainted with the smell of human flesh! Tell me, who have you hidden here? I want to know, or it will go ill with you!"

The giant's wife took fright.

"Do not be angry, dear husband; it is only my brother, who has come to see me. Do not harm him, I beg you!"

"Then why did you not tell me at once? If he is your brother, then he is my brother-in-law, and why should I harm him? Let him show himself!"

The giant leapt up and embraced his brother-in-law until all the bones in Malo's body creaked. Then the giant asked him how he had got to the mansion-house.

"Since morning I have been following a silver hare. I wanted to catch him and let him go in the garden, but he was too clever for me. In the end I tried to shoot him, but I could not even manage that," Malo admitted. "Tomorrow I shall try again."

"Forget the hare, and stay here with your sister instead!" laughed the giant. "Brother-in-law, I have been hunting him for five hundred years, and I still have not caught him!"

But Malo was not to be put off.

"Maybe tomorrow my luck will change," he said.

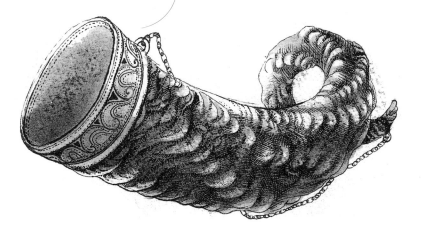

The giant took down an ivory hunting-horn from the wall and handed it to Malo.

"If you insist, then at least I shall come to your aid when you call me. You have only to blow on this horn, and wherever in the whole wide world I may be, in a moment you will find me by your side."

The young man thanked the giant; then he sat up a while with them, and after a brief sleep rose early in the morning and took his leave of his sister and her husband.

"Do not forget my horn!" the giant called after him.

The hunter wandered and blundered through the thicket, until suddenly something glittered before his eyes, as if a silver ball were rolling along in front of him.

"Ah! There you are!" he called out, joyfully. But his joy was misplaced, for the hare led him along all day, up hill and down dale, through thicket and thorn. As evening fell, the exhausted Malo sighed at last, "I suppose I shall spend the night in the forest, and in the morning I shall continue on my way."

"Why should you spend the night in the forest, when just beyond the thicket lies the mansion of your middle sister?" the hare said in a human voice.

And all was as it had been the day before. He arrived in front of an old mansion-house and banged on the gate, and when his sister heard his voice she was beside herself with joy. She embraced her brother, and hugged him close, but then sighed, like her elder sister.

"Dear brother, I am afraid for you. In a while my husband will return, and who knows if he might not harm you. He is not wicked, but he is a powerful giant. He eats twelve oxen at one meal, and I truly never know what such a strange fellow is capable of . . ."

The middle sister also hid her brother behind some barrels, but to no avail; the moment the giant took a draught of wine from his silver bucket, he cried out, "Wife, the wine is tainted with the smell of human flesh! Tell me who you are hiding here, or it shall be the worse for you!"

When the giant heard that her brother had come to see her, he calmed down at once and greeted his brother-in-law; it was a wonder he did not grind the lad's bones to powder in his joy. And when [42] he heard that Malo had been pursuing the silver hare for three days, he almost split his sides laughing.

"Give up hunting the hare, and stay with your sister instead," he told him, at last. "Brother-in-law, I have been hunting him for seven hundred years, and have never caught him."

But Malo was not to be discouraged this time either.

"Maybe tomorrow I shall have better luck," he replied.

The giant took down a large bird's beak from the wall.

"If it must be, then I shall come to your aid whenever you call me. You have only to whistle on this bird whistle, and wherever I may be in the whole world, in a moment you will find me by your side."

The young man thanked the giant, and after sleeping for a while he rose early in the morning and took leave of his sister and his brother-in-law.

After a long trek, it was no longer a surprise for Malo to find that the hare had led him to the home of his youngest sister, again as night was falling. She greeted him as had the other two, with great joy, and her husband welcomed him with open arms. And when Malo told them how he had been taken to them by the hare, which he had been chasing for a whole three days, the giant roared with laughter until the walls of the old mansion began to shake.

"Brother-in-law, I have been hunting the silver hare for a thousand years. Just when I think I have him, he disappears before my eyes like a puff of smoke. But I have not seen him for a long while, and thought he had gone off somewhere. Do not worry your head over the hare; you would do better to stay here with us: your sister will be pleased, and you shall want for nothing."

"I should gladly join you here," Malo replied, "but I should like to try once more to catch the hare tomorrow." At that his brother-in-law gave him a lock of golden hair, promising to come to his aid whenever he pressed it in his palm.

Early the next morning, with a heavy heart, Malo took leave of his relatives and went off again to seek the silver hare. He found it not far away among the bushes, as if it were waiting for him there. And once again the hare led him through thicket and thorn, until suddenly the gleaming waters of the sea opened up before him.

"Now at last I have you!" cried Malo, gleefully, but his joy was premature. All at once the hare leapt from the cliffs into the sea — but then it ran along the water as if it were still on dry land, as swift as you please, until it disappeared in the distance like a patch of mist.

The hapless young man searched desperately for some kind of boat, but in vain: the coast was deserted. At last he spotted a stone cottage tucked between two large rocks. He stepped inside, and found an old cobbler sitting beside the window.

"Good day, old man," Malo greeted him. "Did you by any chance see a silver hare a moment ago? He escaped from me, and ran across the water as if he were on dry land, then disappeared in the distance like so much mist."

"I saw nothing," replied the cobbler.

"I have been hunting the hare for three days, through thicket and thorn, and would give a great deal to know where he is now," sighed Malo.

"In that case I shall tell you something, sir. You might chase that silver hare in vain your whole life; you would never catch him. For it is no hare, but the daughter of the King of Persia, who is enchanted; I am her shoemaker. Every day I sew her two pairs of silver shoes, and I always take them to the palace for her myself."

"Old man, I will give you whatever you ask, if you take me with you," Malo begged him.

"I want for nothing; but it is a hard task which you set yourself, young sir," replied the cobbler. "Many have lost their lives in trying to set the princess free. And truly I cannot help anyone to enter the palace, for it would go ill with me."

All the rest of the cobbler's words were quite lost on the young man. Now that he had heard that the old man was to go to the palace, he begged him over and over again to help him to get there. He swore that he would hide himself well in the palace of the Persian king, and that if they should find him, he would never reveal who had taken him there, even if it cost him his life. In the end the old man relented. He gave Malo a cloak which made him invisible the moment he put it on. Then he, too, wrapped a great cloak around [44]

himself, took Malo on his back, and flew up into the air. They flew like the wind across the open sea, and landed right in the palace of the King of Persia.

"And now you must take care, young sir!" the cobbler whispered to him. "Follow me, quietly and carefully, and be sure not to give yourself away! While you are wearing the cloak, no one can see you, but they can hear you well enough."

The invisible young hunter wandered quietly about the palace; he saw many treasures there, walls lined with gold and silver, precious objects at every step, but not a living soul anywhere. It was not until evening that, as if out of nowhere, large numbers of servants and courtiers, young and old, appeared.

After dark the princess came running along from under the sea, and at that moment the whole palace brightened, like when the evening star appears in the sky. But the face of the princess was sad, and tears gleamed in her eyes like precious stones.

"Yesterday I saw my loved one for the last time," she lamented to her old nurse. "Today I searched in vain for him all day long."

The old woman did her best to comfort the girl.

"Do not worry, my lady, you are sure to find him again. Now you had better have something to eat and take a rest, for you have been running about the world all day, and you are surely tired."

The beautiful princess scarcely touched the fine delicacies which were set before her on golden plates — while Malo's mouth watered, for he was by now ravenous with hunger. When at last all was quiet and he was left alone with the princess, he summoned up his courage and whispered to her, "Beautiful princess, you have eaten and drunk, but I am famished."

The princess was so startled she nearly fell over backwards.

"Who are you, and where are you?" she cried. "I can't see any-one!"

Malo flung the cloak from his shoulders, and at that moment the young hunter stood before his beloved princess, and the two of them smiled happily at each other.

Early the next morning, the princess went to speak to her father.

"Father, dear father; you know I must run to the forest now. But

[46]

first tell me: now that I shall be enchanted only one more year, might I get married?"

"You might, and yet you might not," sighed the old king. "For none has yet come to ask for your hand; all of them have perished on the way."

Then the Persian princess told her father how a hunter from the coast of Brittany had pursued her day after day, and finally, after much searching, had found her across the sea.

"Very well, my daughter; I should gladly accept such a young man as my son-in-law, were he prepared to wait here with me for the whole of the last year of our enchantment. But he may not step outside the walls of the palace while you are wandering the world in the form of a hare. I tell you, it will be a hard time for both of you; your young man will eat his heart out for you more than once."

Malo agreed to all this, though it truly made him sad. All day long he would only walk about the gardens or wander around the palace, waiting for his dear princess to come home in the evening and to change back from a hare into a beautiful woman; waiting for all to come to life again at night.

By and by he knew his way around the whole palace, and he was tormented by anxiety. His heart was heavy when he thought of his loved one, roaming about through all manner of thickets, wary of danger at every step. As he was wandering about the chambers with his troubled thoughts, he heard some sort of din. He walked through all the rooms, peered into the courtyard, and walked back and forth across the garden, but he could find nothing. But at the end of the garden the noise seemed to get louder. At that instant he forgot the words his wife had spoken to him the night before their wedding: "If you are able to stay in the palace and the gardens for a year and a day, without setting foot outside, then I shall never change into a hare again, and we shall all be released from the spell. But the moment you take a single step outside the palace walls, we are all lost."

Lost in thought, and wishing to see what was going on outside the wall, Malo opened a gate, and saw right in front of him the entrance to a cellar. As soon as he opened the door a crack, a devil came rushing out.

"Thank you, young fellow, for setting me free. I was beginning to think you would never come! From now on your wife is mine. Fare you well — I am going to fetch her!" he chuckled.

"Hey, wait a moment!" cried Malo, beside himself with horror. "Is she not yours because I set you free? Then at least give me one single day in order to take my leave of her!"

"Very well, as you wish," snapped the devil. "You can keep her for another day. But remember: at noon tomorrow I shall come for the princess and take her away."

With that the devil was gone: he must surely have fallen straight into hell. With a heavy heart Malo went back to the palace; it was a wonder he did not tear all his hair out with grief. The moment his wife saw him that evening, she knew that something was wrong. She turned as pale as death.

"Malo, dear husband; do not tell me that you went out of the garden and set the devil free?" she asked, wringing her hands.

"Forgive me, dear wife: I heard a noise as if the walls would fall down. I do not even know how I got outside. I only wanted to find out what was happening. But do not be afraid: I shall not let the devil take you. I shall drive him back into hell."

The next day at noon the devil came whistling into the palace.

"Where is the Persian princess?" he growled at Malo.

"She is here; she is just dressing," called Malo from upstairs. "Go to the lawn in front of the palace, and I shall bring her to you in a moment."

The devil went to wait in front of the palace, and in a while Malo came out with the princess. They had scarcely set foot outside the gate, when the devil thrust out his hand to grab her. But Malo was quicker: in a flash he put to his lips his brother-in-law's hunting horn, and blew a loud blast. At once all the horned animals from every corner of the earth appeared, and set about the devil. They poked him and butted him and gored him, until it was a wonder they did not rip him apart. The devil roared with pain. In the end he called out, "I shall be back again tomorrow!" And he was gone.

When the devil came the next day, Malo blew on the second brother-in-law's whistle, and flocks of birds attacked the devil. They scratched him and pecked him, until it was a wonder they did not put his eyes out. It would surely have been the end of him, had he not disappeared into thin air, calling out as he did so that he would be back again the next day.

"Very well, but for the last time!" Malo called after him. "If you show your face again after tomorrow, you shall not escape with your life!"

The third day at noon the Breton hunter was waiting for the devil; he had with him not only the princess, but also his brother-in-law's lock of hair. As soon as he squeezed it, all the haired animals of the earth came running, and laid into the devil with their teeth, fangs, tusks and claws. He tried in vain to defend himself, but they would not let go of him, and would have made an end of him, if he had not signed with the blood of his little finger a promise that from then on he would stay in hell, and would never pursue the Persian princess again. Then the torn and battered demon vanished forever, and at that instant everything came to life as if by the wave of a magic wand. No tongue can tell the joy that reigned all about, now that the spell was broken.

The King of Persia invited the noblemen of the whole world to a wedding feast, and for a whole three years they feasted and made merry. Malo's sisters came, too, together with their husbands — three handsome princes, who had also been released from their spell. They all thanked Malo, and from then on all lived in happiness and contentment, and are living so to this day, if they have not died.

Jamie and the Sleeping Beauty

There once lived a poor widow who had nothing but her only son, a simple cottage on the edge of the village, and a tiny patch of land. But despite their great poverty, her heart would glow with joy whenever she looked at her boy. Jamie was a hard-working lad; before he was very old he had begun to pasture the sheep, and he would lend a hand here, run an errand there. If he earned a penny for his pains, he took it straight to his mother. And so they lived together in peace and contentment. I daresay they would be living so to this day, if Jamie had not happened to glance up one day and see a light shining from the mansion up on the hill. He set out towards it, and all at once he heard the sound of a merry song coming from the old house.

The mansion-house had seen better days. Once it had been the home of mighty lords, but for years now it had lain deserted; its win-

dows were broken, and half the slates were missing from the roof. Down in the village they used to say the little folk had moved in there.

Jamie was seized with curiosity. He had seen the light on the hill, heard the singing; but he could not imagine what might be going on in the half-ruined mansion.

One summer's evening — it was Midsummer's Eve, as it so happened — Jamie again heard singing coming from the old house, and saw a light shining on the hill. This time he couldn't resist: up he jumped, ran out of the cottage, and made a beeline towards the light. A merry singing, laughing and whooping came drifting down from the mansion-house. When Jamie heard it, he supposed he might have a good time with such a happy crew, and strode boldly on. Passing through the gate, which was off its hinges, he crossed the courtyard and entered the great hall of the mansion. There the tables groaned beneath the weight of all the food and drink, and pipers were playing for all they were worth. Little people, scarcely more than a span in height, were sitting at the tables, eating and drinking, and tiny lads and lasses twirled nimbly as they danced across the floor.

As soon as Jamie appeared in the doorway, he was greeted by a chorus of merry voices:

"Welcome, Jamie; welcome among us!"

The pixies leapt to their feet and led Jamie to the head of the table. They treated him as an honoured guest, bringing him as much to eat and drink as he could wish for, and Jamie had such a fine time at the mansion-house that the thought of setting off back home never even crossed his mind.

Then midnight struck. The musicians fell silent, and the little folk jumped up from their tables, all shouting at once.

"To the royal city! Let us to Dublin to fetch the most beautiful of maidens! Come with us, Jamie!"

"Indeed I shall, if you will take me!" called Jamie, and he strode towards the door.

There were horses waiting in the courtyard. Jamie leapt into the saddle, and his mount soared into the sky as if on mighty wings. He had scarcely caught a glimpse of his cottage home beneath him, when he found himself miles away from the village. He looked down on hills and valleys, rivers and lakes, meadows and hamlets. Whenever they flew over a town or a village, a river or a mountain, the pixies called out where they were. Soon Jamie's head was spinning from all these strange names. Suddenly they all shouted:

"Dublin! Dublin! Dublin!"

Slowly and silently, they came to earth in front of a great palace. Beyond an open window a young girl as lovely as a dream lay sleeping. The moment Jamie set eyes on her, he was unable to look away.

The pixies had no trouble at all in climbing up to the bedchamber and lifting the sleeping maiden as she lay. Between the white sheets in her stead they thrust a log of wood. In an instant it changed into a woman, whose face was exactly the same as that of the stolen maiden.

The pixies jumped back onto their horses, rose into the air, and flew off home. They passed the girl from one to the other; first she was held by the one who led them, then by the one behind him, and so on, so that she got nearer to Jamie all the time. When they had nearly reached his home village, the lad spoke up:

"Why do you not give the girl to me for a while? You have all carried her now."

"All right, Jamie, your turn has come."

Jamie hugged the sleeping beauty tightly and flew down with her to his mother's cottage door.

"You thieving rascal!" shouted the little folk, at the top of their voices. "Would you rob us of the most beautiful maiden in the whole of Ireland?" And they flew after the lad like a swarm of angry wasps.

But Jamie did not let go of the girl, though the pixies changed her with waves of their wand into a black dog, a red-hot iron, a sack of wool, and all manner of other things. In the end their magic was exhausted, and she got back her true form. Then the oldest of the pixies shrieked:

"Very well, have her if you must! But she will bring you no great joy! Hear you: from this day on, your maiden shall be quite deaf [52] and dumb!" With that he raised his hand and once more cast a spell over the girl.

Jamie let out a loud cry: the pixies disappeared, and the boy's startled mother appeared in the doorway.

"What is it, my son? Where have you been all night, and what is that you are carrying?"

"I have been in the mansion-house, and out in the wide world, and I have here the most beautiful girl in the whole of Ireland."

"But what are we to do with her?" cried his mother. "Upon my word, she is not from a poor cottage such as ours. Her hands are as white as snow, and her nightgown of embroidered silk."

"But she is a hundred times better off here with us than up in the mansion-house with the little folk."

The poor woman shook her head, threw her shawl around the girl, and hurried over to the old chest, where she took out her own wedding gown. When the girl had put it on, she was as pretty as a picture.

"And what now?" Jamie's mother fretted. "What will she eat? How will she live here, poor thing?"

"Do not worry, mother. She will be a hundred times better off than with the little folk in the mansion-house. And I shall do the work of two."

From that day on Jamie worked even harder than he had done before, and the dumb girl, too, helped about the house, and sewed and embroidered so beautifully that it was a wonder to see what loveliness appeared beneath her fingers. So it was that a year passed quickly by in the little cottage.

It was Midsummer's Eve again when the sound of singing floated down from the mansion-house once more. Jamie crept out of the cottage, hoping he might somehow find out at the mansion how to release his loved one from the terrible spell.

He walked around the walls, and suddenly heard the pixies recalling his visit the year before.

"Oh, how much fun it was with Jamie last year! The fool thought he had got the better of us, and now he has a deaf and dumb sweetheart at home. And yet all it would take would be three little drops of what I am drinking, and at once she would be able even to hear the grass grow, and could sing like a bird."

That was all Jamie needed. He waited outside a good while, then, putting on a bold front, he walked into the great hall. In fact his heart was thumping and his knees felt like jelly, but he did not let the little people see how frightened he was. Nor did they show any sign of being angry with him. They greeted him with merry cries and singing.

"Come and join us, Jamie! Eat and drink with us — come and make merry!"

Jamie strode up to them, but he did not sit down at the table. He picked up a full goblet, as if to drink a toast with the pixies, but as they all raised their goblets to their lips, he suddenly grabbed the one from which the oldest of them was drinking, and shot out of the house with it like an arrow from a bow. The pixies screamed with rage and set off after him. Jamie ran for his life, the goblet clutched tightly in his hands and the pixies hard on his heels. Over hedge and ditch he leapt, making for his mother's cottage at the foot of the hill. When he got home at last, where the little folk had no more power over him, nearly all the precious liquid had been spilt. Only three drops were left in the goblet.

Jamie woke up the sleeping girl and gave her the three drops of the pixies' beverage to drink. From that instant she was able to hear and speak as well as before. She wept with joy, and sat talking to Jamie and his mother until dawn, telling them who she was and speaking of her life at home in Dublin. When daylight came, the girl got up and said, "Now I must go back to Dublin. My parents are surely grieving for me."

"But how will you get there, my child? We have no money for the coach, and you cannot walk so far," Jamie's mother told her.

"I shall walk there, if Jamie will help me again," the girl replied.

Early the next morning, Jamie threw a bundle on his back and took leave of his mother, and when the girl had thanked her tearfully for her kindness, they set out on the long road to Dublin.

The way was as tiresome as it was long, but in the end they reached the city safely. They stopped in front of the great palace and banged at the gates. When a servant came to the window, the girl ordered him:

"Sean, tell the master his daughter has returned."

"My master has no daughter," the servant replied. "He had one, a beautiful girl, but she died a year ago."

"Sean, do you not recognize me?" the girl asked in dismay.

The old servant shook his head, but he sent a page to bring the master at once.

Before long the lord himself was standing in the doorway.

"Father, dear father!" the girl cried, joyfully.

"How dare you call me father! I have no daughter, nor ever had one such as you," he said, proudly, and was about to have the pair of them driven from his door.

"Call the mistress!" cried the girl, weeping bitterly.

At first the lord would not hear of it, but in the end he had the mistress sent for.

"Mother, surely you must recognize me!" the girl lamented, stretching out her arms towards her mother.

The grief-stricken mother raised her head, took a good look at the girl, dressed as she was in poor peasant's clothes, and then opened her arms wide.

"My child!"

What a homecoming it was! All the neighbours gathered round, and Jamie and the girl had to tell them all the story of what had happened the year before, and how Jamie had set the maiden free.

For three days Jamie only rested, feasted and talked about his adventures; he admired all the beauties of Dublin, but in the end he began to make ready for the journey home. They tried in vain to dissuade him; Jamie told them that his mother was waiting for him, and a great deal of work besides.

"If you go, then I shall go with you," said the girl, and she held out her hand to Jamie.

"Is there not room enough in the palace for all?" her parents asked. And at once they sent a carriage for Jamie's mother.

After that they all lived in happiness and contentment in famous [55] Dublin town.

Big-Eyes

Once upon a time, a widow and her three sons lived in a cottage below the forest. One day in winter, when it was snowing heavily, the woman wanted to bake some scones. But when she went to stoke up the fire, she saw that there were only a few logs left.

"Go into the forest and fetch some brushwood," she told her eldest son.

The young lad didn't feel like getting up from the bench and going out into the blizzard, but in the end his mother pushed him out of the cottage. No sooner had he taken a few steps outside the door, than he sank to his waist in snow. As soon as he had crawled out of the drift, he hurried home and sat down again by the fire. He wasn't going to perish in a snowstorm over a bundle of firewood.

The last of the logs burned slowly away, the embers died, and it was a long time till morning. The middle son grunted something or other, got up, and went out to bring some wood from the forest. He waded through the deep, soft snow, looking for dry trunks to cut down, so that he might have fuel enough to take home. Suddenly, he saw a tall wooden watchtower, though he had never seen one in that place before. He walked round it, looking for the entrance, so that he might take a look inside, but he could find none. He walked round it once more, and when he looked more carefully, he saw a single small window beneath the roof. Just then, the window opened, and a large head appeared, with great, flat eyes, each the size of a man's fist.

"Hey there, young fellow," said the big-eyed one, "please help me! Bring me a little water. The spring is only a short way from here, and you will find a jug there. As you can see, I cannot get out of here, and I am terribly thirsty."

"What will you give me?" asked the young man.

"I have nothing to give," replied the old man. "I will reward you with a kind word."

"Then you can find a way to help yourself!" retorted the lad. "What use to me are your kind words? I need to find firewood quickly, so that we do not freeze to death."

As the middle brother turned away from the big-eyed one, a stick suddenly jumped out of the snow and gave him a sound thrashing. When he tried to leap out of the way, he landed in a patch of briars which dug their thorns into him until he cried out with pain. By the time he ran out of the forest, he was battered and torn, and scared out of his wits. At last, half dead, he tumbled into his mother's cottage.

"What has happened, my son?" cried the widow. "Whatever is the matter?"

"Woodreeves!" mumbled the shamefaced youth. "There were woodreeves in the forest, and they would not let me either cut dry trees or gather brushwood. They shouted at me and beat me, and drove me out of the forest!"

"Woe is me!" lamented the poor old woman. "We have neither a fire to keep us warm, nor a morsel to eat. We shall starve to death!"

Then the youngest son stood up.

"I shall go into the forest to try my luck. Maybe I shall have better fortune."

David — for that was the name of the youngest son — went out of the cottage, waded through the deep snow, and in a while came to the tall watchtower in the forest. He was greatly surprised to find it there, and once again the window opened, and the old man called out to him, "Hey, young fellow, please help me! I am terribly thirsty. A little way from here there is a spring, and you will find a jug there. Go and fill it for me; you can see that I cannot get out."

"Very well," David agreed. He was hard put to push his way through the deep drifts, and the spring turned out to be a good distance away, but by and by he returned with the jug, full of water.

Big-eyes let down a piece of string from the window. The lad tied the jug to it, and the old man hauled it up, thanked David, and shut the window.

[57] The lad quickly gathered up a bundle of brushwood. He was just

about to tie it up, so that he might get back home with it as soon as possible, when he became curious. He turned around, and almost froze with horror. The watchtower had disappeared, as if it had never been there at all. At that moment he heard a voice.

"David!"

The lad turned towards the voice, and saw a manikin standing there, dressed in royal robes.

"I am the King of the Forest," said the big-eyed manikin. "A wicked wizard imprisoned me in the tower. But you broke his spell when you took pity on me in my plight. Now I am free again!"

And the forest king took a ring from his finger and gave it to David.

"My son, whenever you need anything, you have only to slide my ring along your finger, and your every wish will be fulfilled."

"Thank you kindly, Your Majesty," said David, bowing to the king. And he slipped the ring into a leather purse. Then the King of the Forest vanished among the trees, and David walked back over to his bundle of firewood. Before he even touched it, it tied itself up as neatly as you please and would almost have jumped up on his back. It was as light as a feather on the way home.

David's mother was pleased when the lad arrived home with such a pile of dry wood.

"Now we shall be nice and cosy!" she cried, joyously. In a little while the cottage was warm again.

At the top of a hill, not far from the widow's cottage, stood a great mansion, the home of a mighty lord. He had once lived a merry life, but recently he had been afflicted by great misfortune. A powerful witch had taken all his riches from the mansion. She had put all the gold, silver and precious stones from the lord's coffers and purses into a huge sack, and taken them into a deep cellar which was let into the rock beside the mansion. Then she had lit a huge fire in front of the great iron door. The flames of the witch's fire leapt high into the sky, day and night. No one was able to put out the magic flames, not with water, nor with sand, nor with anything in the world. Nor was anyone able to pass through them. Thus it was impossible to get into the cellar.

Soon the lord declared that he would give his daughter's hand in marriage to anyone who was able to get the sack with his money and other riches out of the cellar. He would also give the bridegroom one third of the wealth as a dowry. Young men from near and far hurried to the mansion to try their luck, for the lord's riches were great, and his daughters were famed for their beauty. But all was in vain. The less courageous of them gave up as soon as they saw the fearful blaze, while the bolder ones who tried to jump across the rocks were burnt before they got anywhere near the cellar.

David's elder brothers, too, went along to the mansion, but they were afraid of the flames.

"Now I shall try my luck," said David, one day.

"Don't make a fool of yourself," sneered his eldest brother. "There's plenty have tried, and come to a sticky end."

His mother grieved sorely. "I have seen that terrible fire with my own eyes: no man alive is able to jump through it. You will only meet your death in the flames, if you go there."

But David was not to be dissuaded, and made his way straight to the lord's cellar. There he slipped on the forest king's ring and wished that no fire might burn him. Then he strode boldly through the flames without so much as singeing his clothes. He soon found the sack, but it was so heavy he could scarcely lift it to his shoulders to carry it back through the fire. Once again he passed through the licking flames unharmed.

He took the sack into the courtyard of the mansion, dropped it in front of the gate, and made off as fast as his legs could carry him.

But the lord and his three daughters were looking out of the window, and they saw David.

"Who is that ragged fellow, and what is in the sack he threw down before our gate?" the lord asked in wonder. None of his daughters was able to answer him. But the youngest thought to herself: he must be very poor, but he is very handsome, too.

The servants came to say what was in the sack, and at that moment there was a great noise and fuss in the mansion.

"The gold, the stolen gold and silver from the lord's coffers!" shouted one above the other.

Meanwhile, David had returned home. Now he knew the real worth of the ring he had hidden in his purse. And he thought to himself how they might have a fine house instead of their poor cottage. And that his mother, his brothers and he might always be happy.

At that moment, all that he wished for came true. His mother and his brothers were left speechless, their eyes almost popping out with wonder. They thought it must be just a pleasant dream. But David did not show them the ring, or tell them how the King of the Forest had rewarded him for setting him free.

Soon they were all sitting at table to enjoy their new-found good fortune. They were afraid it would all disappear before their eyes like the morning mist.

The lord wasted no time in sending servants north, south, east and west in search of the young man who had brought the sack. By and by they came to the house of the widow, and recognized David at once, even in his fine new clothes. They took to their horses and galloped off to tell their master. The lord sent his finest carriage, drawn by four black horses, to fetch David, and before very long it was drawing up at the mansion door.

"Welcome, my son," said the lord, as the carriage pulled up.

"Welcome, David!" said all three of his daughters, smiling. The youngest of them must surely be the most beautiful maiden in the whole wide world, thought David to himself. When she looked at him, he slipped the ring a little way along his finger, inside the purse, and wished that she might fall in love with him.

And the lord's youngest daughter did indeed fall in love with David from that moment on — for had she not liked him the moment she first saw him out in the courtyard?

Before long there was a wedding to surpass all weddings at the mansion. The guests ate and drank and danced and sang for a whole seven days, from morning till night and from night till morning.

As soon as the wedding feast was over, David thought how he would like to live in a beautiful new mansion. As soon as the guests had departed, the young couple moved into the most beautiful mansion in the whole of the kingdom, and lived there happily, along with David's mother and brothers.

Diarmuid Redbeard the Magician

Once, very long ago, there lived in Ireland a rich farmer who had a single son. From an early age the lad seemed to be very clever, so they sent him to school until he was twenty-one years old.

When at last the young man returned from his school far away, everything in his home and around it seemed new and strange. The first person to catch his eye was a new servant-girl in the kitchen. No one knew her family, for she had come from some village in a far-off part of the land. She did her work with great skill, and was liked by all at the house.

The very first morning after his return, the lad went to look over his father's lands. He climbed a hill from which there was a good view of the fields and meadows. Suddenly he saw in front of him a little old man with a long, fire-red beard. The young man greeted him, and the bearded fellow stopped to have a chat with him. He asked about one thing and another, and in the end enquired whether the boy would not play at least one game of cards with him.

"Why not?" replied the student. "We passed the time at school that way often enough."

The old man pulled a pack of cards out of a leather bag, and all of a sudden placed a golden table and silver stools in the middle of the meadow. Before the startled young man could come to his senses, he was sitting at the table, and the game began. They played and played while the sun shone, and when their game came to an end, they saw that evening was falling. When they had counted up, they found that the young man had won.

"I see you are a clever young fellow," said the old man. "What would you like in payment?"

"I can see that you know many things," replied the student, "therefore I should like my father's meadows to be filled with so many sheep that not even a needle might fall to the ground between them."

"It would be kinder of you to ask something which I might be able to fulfil," retorted the old man.

"I know well enough that you can fulfil what I ask."

"Very well, then take a look around you!" the old man told the young. The student leapt from the table in surprise, for his father's meadows were completely covered with snow-white sheep. There really were so many of them that not even a needle could have fallen down between them. The boy turned back towards the old man, but he was nowhere to be seen. He had vanished as if he and his golden table had fallen into the ground. But when the young man's eyes turned towards the sheep again, they too were gone. There was not a single white sheep grazing there any more. The lad shook his head and set off slowly home. In the courtyard he met the new servant-girl.

"Where have you been so long? Everyone has been looking for you, for you have been gone all day."

The young man told the servant-girl how he had met the strange old man with the red beard, and how they had played cards together until evening.

"And who won?"

"I did."

"And what forfeit did you ask?"

"Not much. Only for there to be so many sheep on my father's meadows that a needle could not fall down between them."

"And where are the sheep?" she asked in surprise.

"I do not know. They disappeared before my eyes. And the old man and his golden table disappeared too, as if the earth had swallowed them up."

"I shall give you some advice, and you would do well to take it. Do not walk about your father's lands alone any more, so that you may not meet the old man again. If you keep out of his way, all will be well; if not, he will be the ruin of you."

The student thought these were just the idle words of a frightened servant-girl, and the next morning he set out even earlier for the hill where he had met the old man with the fiery beard.

The old man seemed to be waiting for him: the table and the cards were ready.

"Shall we play again today?" he asked the young man.

"Why not?" replied the student.

They played while the sun shone, and when they had finished their game, they again saw that evening had come. They counted up, and found that the young man had won again.

"I see that you have indeed a wise head on your shoulders," the old man praised him. "Tell me what you would like today in return for your victory."

"I should like there to be golden ships on the sea as far as I can see."

"Hm," said the old man, "don't you think you are asking a little too much of me? It would be kinder of you to ask for something I can fulfil."

"I have seen well enough that you know many things," replied the student. "I am sure you can grant my wish."

"Very well; take a look around you."

The student looked down from the hilltop towards the sea, and as far as his eyes could see there was not even the tiniest patch of sea without a golden ship bobbing up and down upon it. The young man gave a gasp, and turned round. Lo and behold, there was no

sign of the old man or his table. His eyes turned back towards the sea, but he saw only the waves, with their white crests. There was not a ship in sight. He shook his head, and walked slowly back home. The new servant-girl was waiting for him in the courtyard.

"Where have you been so long?" she asked.

"I have been sitting on the hilltop, playing cards."

"And who won?"

"I did, but I have nothing to show for it," the young man owned, and he told her the whole story.

"And why did you not demand at once that the ships must stay on the sea, after what happened to the sheep yesterday?" the girl asked.

The student did not answer; he only hung his head in silence.

"Don't you see that the old man will soon be the ruin of you?" the girl went on. But the student took no heed of her words, and rose at dawn. By sunrise he was up on the hill. The old man was waiting, as if they had agreed to meet there. They played and played, without taking so much as a bite to eat, until the sun set. Then they counted up, and this time they found that the young man had lost.

"What do you ask as a forfeit?" the young man said. He was beginning to regret that he had not taken the servant-girl's advice, for all of a sudden he had grown terribly afraid of the red-bearded old man.

"A mere trifle!" laughed the old man, and it was a laughter that made the young man's blood freeze. "Only that within a year and a day you find the house of Diarmuid Redbeard, in the land of Nowhere. If you are really clever, then you will find it. If not, then you shall not rest day or night; you shall never eat twice at the same table, or sleep twice in the same bed. Fare you well," he chuckled, and vanished along with his table and stools.

The young man made his way home with a heavy heart. The servant-girl was waiting for him in the courtyard, and when she saw how downcast he looked, she did her best to comfort him, so that he might then tell her what had happened.

"I lost," he said, in the end.

"I knew it could not end otherwise," the girl told him. "What forfeit did he ask?"

The young man told her everything, and the girl nodded her head.

"Do not worry; have a good supper and sleep well. A year and a day is time enough."

Whenever the student wanted to set off in search of the house of Diarmuid Redbeard, the servant-girl always told him there was time enough before the year and a day was up. But in the end he refused to be persuaded, for he was afraid of the old man's curse. He kept it a secret from his parents why he was setting out from his home, telling them he was lonely without his companions from school, and saying that he would visit the nearest of them in a nearby town, just for a day or two. They had no objection, so his mother prepared him a bundle of food and some presents for his friends, and gave him her blessing for the journey, and early the next morning he set off. After he had crossed the courtyard, the servant-girl joined him.

"Here you are setting off, and you have no idea which way you should go!"

"I shall follow my nose, and then perhaps good people will advise me."

"Not even I know the way you must go," the servant-girl said, "or I should have told you long ago. But when I set out into the world, my brother gave me this golden ball to roll in front of me. He told me it would always lead me back to him. Perhaps my brother will know something of Diarmuid, for he is a mighty king in a far-off country. By evening the golden ball will lead you to his castle. It is surrounded by a high wall, and only a single gate leads into the courtyard. It is there that your first difficult task awaits you. Pick up the golden ball, throw it as high as you can into the air, and then jump over the locked gate; when you land in the courtyard you must catch the golden ball again. Remember: it must not touch the ground in the courtyard, otherwise my brother will not help you. And now, farewell, and come safely home."

The lad thanked the servant-girl, and now he set off more boldly into the unknown world. He rolled the golden ball in front of him, and the journey passed quickly until evening. Then, as the dew was falling, the mist rising from the streams, and the cows and horses

making their way from pastures to cowsheds and stables, as the cats were creeping to firesides, and the watchdogs beginning to bark, the golden ball came to a stop in front of a castle gate. The young man looked around, and at once saw the king looking out of a window. The evening breeze stirred his beard and cooled his hot brow. He watched as the farmer's boy picked up the ball and threw it as far as he could in the air, until it disappeared from sight. Then the lad took a run at the tall castle gate, jumped over it first time, and held out his hands and caught the golden ball as it fell.

The king saw with his own eyes how easily the lad had leapt over the gate of the castle, and he called the guards at once.

"I have lived here for one hundred years, and no one has ever been able to jump over the castle gate before. This stranger in the courtyard is the first who has ever done so. He must be some great hero; he will kill or imprison us all, and rule over my kingdom. Take him, and bind him, and then throw him in the darkest dungeon!" cried the king, quite beside himself.

"Wait, wait, noble king!" the young man called. "I am not come to rule over your kingdom, but instead bring greetings from your sister." And he showed the king the golden ball. "It was she who sent me here. This ball rolled in front of me until it led me here."

The king calmed down at once, and ordered his guards to make the lad welcome, and to bring him the golden ball. He examined it carefully, and recognized it at once. He told the guards to halt, and went into the courtyard himself to greet the young man. He was overjoyed to hear from his sister, for he had had no news of her for a hundred years.

Then they spent a third of the night feasting on the finest foods and drinks, a second third in music and dancing, and for the third third they all slept soundly. Three women with shovels collected the ash from their pipes.

In the morning the young man told the king why he had come to him. When the king heard what he was looking for, he shifted on his throne and cleared his throat, but in the end he admitted, "I have ruled here for one hundred years, but I have never heard of Diarmuid Redbeard. Wait a moment, I shall ask my counsellors."

But they, too, knew nothing; they only fidgeted.

"Very well," said the king. "I have an older brother who rules in the next kingdom. The golden ball which led you here will take you there too. But be careful, the wall of his castle is twice as high as that of mine, and you will not be able to enter otherwise than by jumping over the gate."

The young man thanked the king for everything, and set off cheerily after the golden ball. By evening he reached the castle of the elder brother, jumped over the great gate, caught the ball which had brought him there in both hands, and bowed to the king. As soon as the king found out where the lad had come from, he called back the guards at once, so that they might not harm him. He ran to the door himself to greet his guest, so pleased was he to hear greetings from his sister.

"I have ruled here for two hundred years," he sighed, "and in all that time I have not heard from my sister." Then they feasted for a third of the night, danced for another third, and slept soundly for the rest. Seven women with shovels collected the ash from their pipes.

It was only the next morning that the king learned the purpose of his guest's journey. When he heard the name Diarmuid Redbeard, he shook his head.

"I have ruled here for two hundred years," he said, "but I have never heard that name before." Nor were his counsellors any wiser than those of his younger brother.

"There is nothing for it," sighed the king, finally, "but for you to go to our eldest brother. He is king of all animals, birds and fish, and he and his faithful subjects will surely be better able to help you. The golden ball which brought you here will take you to him also; but beware, the gate of his castle is twice as tall as mine, and you will have to jump over it."

The young man thanked the king for everything, and set off after the golden ball with a light heart. By evening it led him to a great castle with a huge wall. The poor student could scarcely see to the top of it, and the gate disappeared into the evening mist. With a sigh, the lad threw the golden ball up into the air with all his might, and jumped as high as he could. He was afraid he was not going to get over the gate, but he did so with his first leap, and caught the ball in his hands. The king was already calling the guards.

"I have ruled here for three hundred years," he cried, "and no one has ever jumped over my castle gate. This stranger is the first to do so. He is surely some hero who will take away my kingdom — bind him, and throw him in the deepest dungeon!"

"Wait, wait!" cried the young man. "I am not come to take your kingdom from you, but bring greetings from your sister and your two younger brothers. It was they who sent me here, and this golden ball rolled before me until it brought me here."

Then the king called off the guard and went to welcome the lad himself, so pleased was he to hear from his sister after all those years. Straight away he had delicacies placed on the table, which they spent a third of the night eating; another third was spent in dancing to fine music, and the remainder in sleeping. Nine women with shovels cleared away the ash from their pipes.

It was not till morning that the king learned why the young man had come. When he heard the name Diarmuid Redbeard, he only shook his head, and the boy grew very sad.

"Do not worry, there is no need to hang your head," the king comforted him. "I have ruled here for three hundred years, and have never heard the name, but that does not mean that we shall not find out everything about him. I am king of the animals, the birds and the fish, I will call them here, and they shall tell us what they know."

The king went into the courtyard and blew on a horn. In an instant the sky darkened with the wings of thousands of birds, the waters boiled with thousands of fish, and the land around the castle was covered with animals, as they made their way to their king. He asked them all about Diarmuid Redbeard, but none knew anything. Then the magpie croaked out:

"The eagle! The old eagle is not here yet! Maybe he will know something."

The king blew his horn once more, and waited; but nothing more ran, or swam, or flew to him. He frowned, and blew yet again, so loudly that his eyes almost popped out of his head. When he took the horn from his lips, a huge eagle was circling just above his head.

"Forgive me, my lord, for coming so late, I was just taking food to my young ones in their nest. As soon as I had fed them, I came."

"Very well," said the king, gruffly. "If you can tell me where the house of Diarmuid Redbeard stands, I shall forgive you at once."

"Where else would it be but in the land of Nowhere, close to my nest?"

"Then I order you to take this young man there."

"If you feed me well, and give the young man food for the journey, that he may feed me on the way, then perhaps I can manage to fly all the way with the lad on my back."

The king fed both the young man and the eagle well, then gave the student a large bag of fish, took his leave of him, and watched as the pair soared into the sky. The eagle flew as swift as the March wind, but in a while he could go on no further. The young man fed him, and the bird again flew more strongly. But by and by the bag of fish was empty, and they were still over the open sea, with the land of Nowhere still out of sight.

"Feed me, feed me, or we shall fall into the sea!" cried the eagle. "You are too heavy; I cannot carry you any more!" he sighed. The young man had nothing at all to give the bird, so in desperation he threw him a piece of his own flesh, torn from his leg. The eagle gained new strength, and soon flew over tall cliffs; he settled on the highest point.

"Here we are, where we want to be," he said. "Jump down from my back, and I will show you where Diarmuid's house is."

The young man climbed slowly and painfully down from the eagle's back.

"What is the matter?" the bird asked. "Was the flight too fast for you?"

"The rapid flight did not harm me, but your hunger," replied the young man. "You ate a piece of my leg, and now I cannot walk."

"Pluck the longest feather from my left wing, and place it against the wound," the eagle told him, "and the pain will stop at once. Then take the longest feather from my right wing, and you will be able to run better than before."

The young man thanked the bird, and he had soon forgotten all [72]

about his pain. Then the eagle showed him a lake down in a valley.

"Can you see those three ducks on the lake?" he asked the student. "Those are the daughters of Diarmuid the magician. Two of them always stay together, and drive away the third, the smallest. Though she is smaller than they are, she is the most skilful. She has to do all the work in and around the house, for their mother, the old witch, likes only the two younger, more beautiful daughters. It is as if the eldest were not her daughter at all. And now look in the bushes," the eagle advised him. "You can see there two white bundles, one larger and the other smaller. The larger one is the clothes of the two younger sisters. Take no notice of them. But the smaller pile is the clothes of the eldest daughter. You must creep up to them and take them. When she finds them gone, she will come after you and ask you to return them. Do not agree to, however she may plead. Tell her you will give her back her clothes only when she promises you she will not only take you into her father's house, but will also lead you safely out again, and protect you while you are there. She will not want to promise at first, but in the end she will agree."

The young man thanked the eagle and took his leave of him. The bird took off, and the young man set out to make the descent into the valley. He took the clothes of the smallest duck from the bushes, shoved them under his arm, and turned his back on the lake. He looked neither to the right nor to the left, but only strode forward, with long steps. Before long he heard a mournful cry.

"I beg of you," a quiet woman's voice addressed him, "I beg you kindly, good young man, give me back my clothes; I should die here in the night on my own, and without my clothes I cannot return home."

For a while the young man pretended not to hear, but the girl pleaded with him so piteously to have mercy on her, that he finally promised to lay the clothes down in the bushes if the girl would promise that she would take him into the house of her father, protect him while he was there, and lead him safely out of it, not allowing the powerful wizard Diarmuid Redbeard to harm him.

"How can I promise that, good sir? My father is mighty, and I am weak; he knows many things, and I know almost nothing."

[74]

"Then promise that you will do all in your power to help me," the young man insisted.

"I promise that I shall always help you, even if I should die along with you," the girl said quietly. Then the young man laid her clothes in the bushes, and the girl told him which path led to the house of Diarmuid Redbeard. She also advised him not to behave quietly and modestly there, but rather to make out that he was the cleverest young fellow in the whole world.

"Thank you," said the young man. "But grant me one more wish. Allow me to turn around, that I may see what you look like when you are not a duck."

"Why should you wish to see me? My two younger sisters have all the beauty, and there is none left for me."

The young man turned quickly, and then shook his head.

"Why did you wish to deceive me?" he asked. "For you have eyes like a mountain lake and hair like the blackest earth. Truly, I like you better that way than if you were to have gold on your head and pride in your eyes."

"Be off with you!" laughed Diarmuid's daughter in a voice as clear as a bell. The young man obeyed, and before long he found himself in front of the magician's house. It was easy enough to get inside, for the door was open wide, and the old man's red beard shone like a blazing fire, though on the hearth only a few embers were smouldering.

"Deary me!" shrieked Diarmuid. "I see you are a smarter fellow than I took you for, since you found your way here."

"Did you really think you were the only one with any wisdom?" retorted the lad, as the girl had told him.

"Oh, what a sharp tongue you have!" laughed the magician. "Well, we shall see, we shall see!"

"Since when has it been the custom to greet guests in such a way?" demanded the lad.

Diarmuid sneered angrily, but he did not reply, for at that moment his three daughters arrived. Two of them were tall and slender, with golden hair hanging down to their knees and pride glazing their eyes. The third was small and dark, and her eyes twinkled.

"What am I to prepare for our guest to eat?" she asked.

"What else but black bread and a little water," snarled Diarmuid. "If he wants better, then he will have to earn it."

But his eldest daughter prepared the young man not only black bread, but also three kinds of meat, gruel and cakes, and not only water, but also ale and mead.

When the time came for them to go to bed, Diarmuid's daughter asked her father, "Where am I to make up a bed for our guest?"

"Where else but in the pantry on the pile of flax stalks?"

But when her father had gone to sleep, the girl made him a bed of silk, with seagull and swan's down. He slept as sweet as could be, until the girl came and woke him up.

"Go quickly into the pantry and lie down on the flax stalks," Diarmuid's daughter told him. "My father will rise in a moment, and he will give you hard work to do. But do not worry; in the evening I shall come home and I will help you."

Before long Diarmuid burst into the pantry where the young man lay.

"Time to wake up, sleepyhead! No one eats under my roof without earning his keep. Get down to work!"

He led his guest into the stables, thrust a fork with one prong into his hands, and ordered him to clean all the dung out of the stables and to find a needle which his great grandmother had dropped there seven hundred years ago.

"If you do not find it before evening," the magician warned him, "you shall be shorter by a head."

The student sighed to think how all his studies had failed to teach him anything about such work as this. He picked up a little dung on the fork and threw it out of the stable, but when he turned around, he saw that twice as much new dung had appeared inside. As evening drew on, there was a good deal more dung in the stable than there had been that morning. How was anyone to find a needle there which had been lost for seven hundred years? As the sun began to sink in the west, the young man felt a strange grip close around his heart. Just then Diarmuid's eldest daughter slipped into the stables, took hold of the fork, and in three tosses emptied the stables of dung. Then she poured clean water on one of the boards, and all of a sudden her great-great-grandmother's needle lay shining at their feet. She handed it to the young man, who did not know how to thank her.

"This was easy work," she told him. "There is harder to come. This needle, too, will come in useful to you. Show it to my father, but do not give it to him when he asks for it."

Now the young man strode boldly through the door and stopped right in front of the wizard. There were only a few embers glowing on the hearth, but Diarmuid's beard burned like fire, so that he needed no light to see his great-grandmother's needle. He frowned like thunder.

"So you have found the needle, have you?" he growled.

"I have indeed," the lad confirmed.

"Then give it to me." The wizard held out his hand.

"The needle is mine; I found it while I was doing the work you gave me."

Diarmuid frowned even more darkly.

"Oh, what a sharp tongue you have! Well, we shall see, we shall see!" he warned. Then he gave orders for the young man to be given black bread and water and for him to sleep on the flax stalks. But the eldest daughter fed him well and made him a bed of down and silk, where he slept as sweet as could be till morning, when the girl woke him up again.

"Get up," she told him. "In a while my father will come, and he will send you to empty the water from the lake with a ladle, and find a ring which my great-grandmother dropped there. But do not fear, this evening I shall help you again," she promised.

And so it was. The lad was given a leaky ladle with which to empty the lake, and to find before evenfall a ring which the magician's grandmother had lost one thousand seven hundred years ago. If he did not, then he would be shorter by a head, the wizard warned him.

By sunset the lad had not even managed to get a panful of water out of the lake with his leaky ladle. He sat down on the bank and waited for his dear friend to come and help him. As the sun sank towards the horizon, his head, too, sank lower and lower; he thought he could see it even now rolling off his shoulders down to his feet, when suddenly he heard a quiet voice.

"Don't worry; here I am, as I promised."

It took only a couple of strokes of the ladle, and all the water in the lake disappeared somewhere or other, leaving a golden ring shining on the dry bed.

"Take it, and hide it well," the girl told him. "Do not let my father get hold of it, and make out that you are wiser than he."

Diarmuid almost split open with rage when he saw the ring on the young man's finger.

"Well, I see that you know more than just how to blow on your porridge. Give me my grandmother's ring, then."

"If you wanted it, then you could have found it for yourself," the lad replied, sharply. "I was the one who picked it up from the dry bed of the lake; therefore it belongs to me."

"Oh, but you'll soon change your tune!" shrieked the magician, and he leapt up from the bench and threw himself into bed without any supper.

The young man ate with relish what Diarmuid's daughter set before him, and slept soundly in his silk sheets until dawn.

"Time to get up," the girl woke him in the morning. "Today my father will give you no work to do, but he will order you to tell him three stories when evening comes. Each must be more interesting than the last, and all three must be so long and so good that he will not sleep a wink from dusk to dawn. But my father will stop up his ears, and you might tell the finest tales in all the world, but he would still fall asleep before long, and in the morning you would lose your head. You must do as I tell you: when my father goes to lie down in the darkened room, place the iron hook against the door, prop the broom up in the corner, and hang the pot over the fire. Then tell them all to begin telling a tale. You must creep outside to the stable, take the bridle which hangs above the door, and shake it. My horse will come running, ready saddled. Jump on him, for I shall be there already, and we shall escape together. Perhaps we shall succeed — if not, we shall die together."

The young man did not feel like dying with Diarmuid's daughter, for he was growing fonder of her all the time. He took good note of what she had told him; he placed the iron hook against the door, the broom in the corner and the pot over the fire, and ordered them to begin their storytelling. Then he was gone. He shook the bridle in front of the stable, and a saddled horse appeared. When he jumped onto it, he saw that his dear one was there already, and off they rode. Their steed flew along with his hooves scarcely touching the ground; he overtook the evening breeze, and carried them far away. Had the horse not been so swift, things might have gone ill with them.

Diarmuid's wife, who was much the same type of witch as he was a wizard, was just returning home from a long journey. She went into the house and heard her husband snoring and the hook, the broom and the pot talking away from inside the closed room.

"What's all this noise?" she shrieked.

"He told us to tell stories, so we are," replied the iron hook from the door.

"Hey, there: get up, lazybones!" The witch roused her husband.

Slowly, the wizard came to his senses, and saw at once what had happened.

"Something indeed, when our eldest daughter has run off with some Irish lout!" shrieked old Diarmuid. And he and his wife set off at once to find the young couple. By morning they had not found them; but the girl was sure they were not going to get away with it so easily, so at dawn she asked the young man to look and see if they were being followed.

"I can see no one, only a pair of ravens seem to be flying after us."

"Faster, good horse, faster — they are catching up with us!" the girl urged her mount. But before long she could hear the beat of the ravens' wings.

"Have you got the needle I gave you?" she asked the young man.

"Indeed," he assured her.

"Then throw it behind us, quickly!"

The lad did as he was told, and in an instant a tall green forest, reaching to the very clouds, grew up behind them. The ravens could not fly so high. They alighted in front of the trees, and Diarmuid said to his wife, "Wife, fly home quickly, and bring me my big hammer. It is lying beside my bed."

The wizard rested for a while, and then there was a flapping of wings.

"Are you flying home, wife?" he asked.

"No, husband, I have returned with the hammer!" croaked the witch.

"Ah, what a clever young thing you are, wife!" he flattered her; then he raised the heavy hammer and flung it into the trees. Wherever it flew it laid the trees to the ground, so that the ravens were able to fly carefully on.

In a while Diarmuid's daughter asked the young man to look behind them again.

"The ravens are coming again!" he cried.

"Have you got my great-grandmother's ring, which you found on the bottom of the lake?"

"Indeed I have."

"Good; then take it from your finger and throw it far away." [80]

He did as he was told, hurling the ring behind his back. At that instant a huge sea, so broad that the ravens could not manage to fly over it, appeared behind them.

"Quickly bring the wooden cup which lies beside my bed," the magician told his wife. And in a moment he heard the beating of wings.

"Are you flying home?" he asked.

"No, husband, I have returned with the cup!" croaked the witch.

"Ah, but you are a clever young thing," Diarmuid praised her. Taking the cup, he went to dry up the sea. But after toiling away for a while, he threw the wooden cup away.

"All to no avail, wife," he said, angrily. "Our daughter has been a good pupil; now she is cleverer than we. Do what we will, we shall not catch them now."

But the witch was not going to give up so easily. Once more she flew high into the air and loudly croaked after her daughter a curse: "May your loved one forget you as you have forgotten us, when he gets home!"

The young man and his loved one now rode on without trouble, and as evening was falling they drew close to the young man's home.

"I shall wait here for you," said the girl, when they reached the hill overlooking the estate. "Go home and tell them whom you have brought with you. But until you call me, do not shake hands with anyone or kiss anyone, for at that moment you would forget me!"

The young man was unwilling to leave his loved one on the hill-top, but he said to himself that he would return for her the moment he had announced his return. As soon as he entered the courtyard, the big dog ran out to meet him, jumped up on him, and licked his cheeks out of joy at seeing the young master again. And at that moment the young man forgot all about his loved one; one after another he shook hands with them all, kissed his mother, rejoiced that he was home again, but gave never a thought to Diarmuid's daughter. On and on the poor girl waited for her loved one, but when she saw that he was not going to come back for her, she cried bitterly, and set off down to the village to find a place to spend the night. But she was afraid of strangers, and in the end she turned her horse loose in the meadows, and climbed into a tree beside the spring, thinking she might wait there till morning. Just then the blacksmith's old wife came down to the spring to fetch water. Leaning over the surface of the spring, the old woman saw a beautiful young face reflected there.

"Oh! How beautiful I am! And didn't even know it!" she shrieked, and, leaving the jug beside the water, ran straight to town. What a shame for such a beauty to spend her life beside the flames of a village smithy's furnace, she thought to herself.

When his wife did not return, the blacksmith sent his elder daughter for water. But she, too, leaned over the water and saw the beautiful face reflected there. Then she ran off to town to go dancing, for what was a good-looking lass like herself doing in a smutty smithy's yard?

When the blacksmith sent his younger daughter to the well, and she, too, did not return, he went along there himself. He bent over, and saw the lovely girl's face reflected in the water.

"Aha!" he cried. "Now I see why I have no water. Come on down from the tree, my lass, and do not be afraid: no one will hurt you."

Thus it was that Diarmuid's daughter went into service at the blacksmith's forge. She cleaned the house, cooked him tasty meals, set the farm in order, and helped out in the smithy from time to time. Indeed, she was able to advise him in blacksmithery in no time at all, so that the smith would not have minded in the least if she had stayed at the cottage for good.

Before long word spread throughout the countryside that the young student from the great farm was to marry the servant-girl. True, no one knew her family, for she was from some distant place, but she was such a good worker and was so pleasant to everyone that all in the household liked her well, and best of all the only son. Rich and poor, young and old from all around were invited to the wedding. Among them were the blacksmith and his new servant-girl. They arrived the evening before the wedding was to take place. There were more people at the house than at a fair in town; pigs and lambs were being roasted in the courtyard, and women were hurrying to and from the oven with bread and cakes. For a while Diarmuid's eldest daughter watched them; then she asked if she might bake a cake of her own.

"Very well," replied the new servant-girl, who was rushed off her feet with work. The girl set to, and baked such a beautiful cake that the servant-girl took it straight to the room where all the most learned men were sitting.

"Mmm, how good it tastes!" they said. "Who baked it?"

"I did," the new servant-girl replied, quickly.

"That is not true!" they said, angrily. "No one in the whole of Ireland can bake a cake such as this one."

Then, like it or not, the servant-girl had to admit that it had been baked by the girl who was in the blacksmith's service.

"Then send her to us!" the learned men replied.

Diarmuid's daughter agreed to go and bow to the gentlemen, but said she must first wash and dress in clean clothes. When she was ready, there was not a woman more beautiful in the whole house. Her hair was like the blackest of earth, and her eyes like the waters of a lake. When she came in, all the gentlemen rose, and asked her to take a seat at the head of the table. The gentlemen talked of this and that, ate, drank and laughed; then the girl asked if weddings were always celebrated thus in those parts.

"Why, of course," they told her. "Is there some other way to celebrate a wedding?"

"In the land of Nowhere, whence I have recently come, different games are played at wedding feasts. Each must do something unusual to entertain the others."

"And would you entertain us with something unusual?" the gentlemen asked.

"Very well, if you so wish; but you should call the bride and groom, for I should like them to see it, too."

So they called in the bride and groom, and the girl drew a golden hen from one sack, and a silver cockerel from another. All gaped when she placed them gently on the table. Then she began to sing a merry song, such as they had never heard before, and the cock and the hen danced on the table. All were amazed at this wonder. When the cock and the hen had finished their dance, the girl tossed three grains of wheat onto the table. The cock ate two of them, leaving only one for the hen.

"Oh, you ungrateful cock!" squawked the hen, angrily. "You would not have been so selfish in my father's house. When I cleaned out the dung from my father's stable and found the needle in the beam, you would gladly have left me two grains. But you have soon forgotten about me!"

Old and young crowded round the table as the girl again began to sing her merry song, and once more the cock and the hen danced on the table. Again the girl rewarded them with three grains of wheat, and again the cock quickly gobbled up two of them.

"Oh, you ungrateful cock!" the hen rebuked him. "You would not have been so selfish in my father's house. When my father ordered you to empty the lake with a leaky ladle, and I did it for you, and gave you the golden ring, you would gladly have left me two grains. But you have soon forgotten about me!"

Everyone laughed, except for the bridegroom, and he grew more and more grave. It seemed to him that he had seen the beautiful girl somewhere before, heard her silver voice. But he could not remember when and where.

Now the girl turned sad eyes on the bride and groom, but still she sang the merry song for the cock and hen to dance to. And when they had danced, again she gave them three grains of corn. Once more, the cock snapped up two of them, and the hen got only one.

"Oh, you ungrateful cock," the hen began again. "In my father's house you would indeed not have been so selfish. That time I taught you how to get a hook, a broom and a pot to tell tales, you would surely have left me two grains. But you have soon forgotten me now, have you not?"

At that the groom turned his back on his bride, and in a couple of strides was beside the wizard's daughter, and embracing her.

"Now I recognize you, my dearest. The dark curse is broken, and now I shall never forget you as long as I live!"

Pandemonium broke out among the wedding guests. When all had calmed down a little, the groom told them the whole story, from beginning to end. At first not even the wisest of them could say whether the young man should marry one bride or the other. Some said: "He should marry the servant-girl. She sent him to her brothers, and they helped him to find the house of Diarmuid Redbeard. If he had not found it, he would have been cursed forever, unable to eat twice at one table or sleep twice under one roof — a homeless vagabond."

"Oh, no!" said others. "This girl does not deserve the bridegroom. She sent him off alone from his home, and he almost went to his death. If Diarmuid's daughter had not helped him, he would have lost his head in the magician's house. Only this girl faithfully came to his aid, and never deserted him. She is the one who deserves that he never desert her."

Then there was the wedding to end all weddings, when the daughter of Diarmuid Redbeard, the magician, married the Irish lad. They lived happily ever after, as did their children and their children's children, to the seventh generation.

The Three Miller's Sons

There was once a miller who had three sons, three fine young fellows. The lads learned their father's trade thoroughly, but there was not too much work in the mill; so the miller was not surprised when, one day, the eldest son said to him, "Father, my brothers and I should like to go out into the world and learn a trade. If you agree, we shall do everything that needs doing about the house, set the mill in order, and set off on our travels."

"Very well, my sons," said the miller. "I should rather one of you stayed at home; but if you have agreed this between you, then I will not stand in your way."

The young men did all that they had promised their father, then early one morning said their farewells, threw their bundles over their shoulders, and stepped out boldly from the mill. They walked and walked alongside a stream, until by and by they came to a crossroads. There they halted, and looked around them to see where they should go now.

"The best thing is for us to go our separate ways," said the eldest. "But first we must promise to meet again at this place in three years to the day."

Then the eldest brother made for a nearby town where, walking along the waterside, he arrived at a mill and asked whether they needed a helper.

"Clever hands can always be put to good use," replied the miller. So the eldest brother quickly put on a miller's apron and threw a sack of grain over his shoulder.

The middle brother's way took him straight into a village, where he came across a tall fence on the outskirts. Beyond the fence a garden stretched as far as the eye could see, and in the middle of the garden a proud mansion, the finest that he had ever seen, reached skywards. Not far from the fence a gardener was mowing grass. The miller's son bade him good day, and asked whether he might not need a helper.

"There is always work for clever hands," replied the old gardener. So the young man took up the scythe, and before the sun set, a full half of the garden was mown, a delight to behold.

The youngest brother went down the road that was left when his brothers had chosen theirs. He walked, and walked, and night had fallen before he reached any habitation. Fortunately he caught sight of a light flickering in the distance.

"Praise be," he said to himself. "I suppose I may spend the night here, and in the morning I shall be on my way again."

The light guided him to a large farm, a long way from any other dwelling.

"Good evening, farmer," he greeted its master. "Might I spend the night on your farm? I have come from afar."

"You may sleep in the barn; we can still spare a slice of bread, and you will find water in the well," replied the farmer, sitting on the bench by the stove. "We are sick and weak, and it goes ill with us." He sighed at each word he spoke.

Even in the dark the young man could see that the farm was large, but neglected. The stable door was off its hinges, the straw in the barn was flung in an untidy heap, and he could scarcely get water out of the well. Early the next morning he leapt up, tidied the yard a little, hung the stable door back on its hinges, and took hay and water to the two sickly cows. When he had done all this, the farmer's wife came out of the house, just managing to hobble along with the aid of a stick.

"Thank you for your kindness in helping us. Things grow worse here day by day, misfortune follows upon misfortune. First of all we lost our seven fine cows, cows such as no one had for miles around. Nor were there many cows in the village at the bottom of the hill, and all the people came to us for milk. We were all healthy, and fit for work. Now we are at death's door, and it seems there will not even be anyone to mourn for us or bury us, for our only daughter is now the poorliest of all. Not long ago she was blossoming like a rose; but now she has withered as if she were smitten by frost. She shivers and shakes, and the fever burns her poor brow."

The young man sighed inwardly, rolled up his sleeves, and got on with some more work. He cleaned out the stable, repaired the well, untied the skinny cows, and drove them into the meadows to graze. Finally, he took the last piece of bread from his pocket; but before he could take a bite, he heard a voice.

"Kind sir, take pity on a poor old woman. Do not allow me to die of hunger: it is four days since even a crust of bread passed my lips."

Yann, for that was the name of the youngest of the miller's sons, was shocked to see an old beggar-woman standing beside a tree, trembling like an aspen leaf. He handed her the piece of bread and, lo and behold! Instead of the beggar-woman, a golden-haired fairy stood before him.

"Do not be afraid, Yann," she said. "I see you are a kind-hearted boy. If you do as I tell you, good fortune shall not pass you by. I know where the seven cows from the farm are. If you drive them back there, everything on the farm will come back to life again; the farmer and his wife will be healthy, as will their daughter, as sweet as honey and as pretty as a flower. All will again be as it was before the water fairy grew angry with them because they did not want their daughter to marry her son — the water dragon."

Finally, the fairy told Yann to take a cudgel from the farmhouse, and to wait for the water fairy at sunset by the bend in the stream. She would speak to him sweetly, and promise him the moon and stars, until she got behind his back. At that moment she would fling him into the wild whirlpool.

"Do not let her get the better of you!" the fairy told Yann. "Pay attention, and throw her in the whirlpool. From that moment on she will be powerless, and will obey your every command. Order her to show you the way to her dragon son, who drove the cows away. When you get near, go quietly, and listen until you hear him breathe out. Then take hold of the cudgel with both hands and make an end of him. Drive the cows back to the farm, and you will scarcely be able to believe all that will happen. Be brave, Yann, and fare you well!"

Yann was afraid no good would come of it all, but he went to fetch the cudgel just the same, flung it onto his shoulder, and waited by the stream. Suddenly he heard a voice as sweet as honey.

"Young fellow, it is a pity to stand there idly, staring into the water, and not lifting a finger, when there is real wealth not three paces away from you. See how much gold there is on the bottom of the stream," the water fairy lured him. Yann did peer into the water, but at the same time he kept an eye on the water fairy, so that she might not fling him into the whirlpool. She was just about to take hold of him, when he jumped deftly out of the way, grabbed the fairy, and threw her into the water. In a moment she surfaced and said in a meek voice, "Tell me what you want of me."

"Where is your son? Where can I find that good-for-nothing dragon?" the young man roared at her.

"How should I know?" she retorted, but in the end she had to show him the way to the dragon's cave, like it or not. Yann set off, and walked for a long while over stones and thistles, until suddenly the dark entrance to the dragon's cave stood before his eyes. He could hear from afar a loud puffing and blowing, like rocks falling down a mountainside. He took a firm grip on the cudgel with both hands, raised it above his head, and went for the dragon like a hornet. The cudgel was only just powerful enough to deal with the dragon. Then Yann quickly drove the seven great cows out of the cave; their coats shone like lanterns on the way. The cows made straight for the farm, and when they got there Yann saw that all was changed beyond recognition. The house and yard were clean, swept and whitewashed, and the farmstead was a delight to behold. The farmer came to the door and greeted Yann like a favourite son, and did not know how to thank him, how to reward him. The farmer's wife wept with joy, and the face of the pretty girl who was standing beside her lit up when she saw Yann. Yann knew at once that he had never even dreamed of a more charming creature in all his life.

Then the people from the nearby village came in droves to buy milk, and took away as much as they could carry; yet there was plenty for everyone. But the rejoicing was even greater when, by and by, Yann married the farmer's daughter, and took over the farm. Want and suffering were driven out of every corner, and they lived very well indeed.

Three years passed in no time, and the day approached when the brothers were to meet at the crossroads. Yann quickly set off towards his home, and he saw from afar that his brothers were waiting for him at the appointed place, watching out for him. The brothers hugged and embraced, slapped each other on the back, and then each told the story of how he had got on in the world.

The eldest brother took out a leather purse, weighed it in his hand, and shook it. Gold pieces rang in it like bells.

"We shall repair the mill, buy one or two things for the farmstead, and shall all live well," he said at last.

The middle brother was not to be outdone; he jangled silver pieces with a sound that was music to the ears.

"But what of you?" they asked the youngest, when he did not show them a purse full of coins. "Have you really nothing to boast about?"

Then the youngest brother nodded towards a loaded waggon standing beneath a tree, with his pretty wife smiling like the spring sun. Around them a herd of cows more beautiful than the brothers had ever seen were grazing. When they heard how their brother had come by his riches and his wife, they could not believe their ears, and there was no end to their questions.

From then on the brothers did not part again. They fetched their father and made their way to Yann's farm. There they farmed and milled in a new mill, and lived so well that they washed in red wine and dried themselves with fine white bread.

The Fruit from the Garden of Vleago

There was once an Irish king who had three sons; but what use was a kingdom to him, when life was wearisome, for the poor fellow was afflicted with a grave disease. Doctors from near and far were consulted day and night, and they tried all the remedies that were ever invented, but nothing made him any better. Then, one day, a wise old man came to the palace and told them that nothing could help the king but to eat his fill three times of fruit from the garden of Vleago, for there was no better remedy in the whole world. But that was all the sage could tell them, so no one had the slightest idea where they should send someone to fetch this precious fruit.

The king's sons were already fully-grown young men. He sent for them, and said, "My sons, I have heard that the only cure for my illness is to eat my fill three times of fruit from the garden of Vleago. But no one knows where this garden is to be found; they know only

that healing fruit grows there, and that there is no better medicine in the whole world. So, dear sons, bring comfort to your ailing father. If my life is dear to you, take the best of the horses from the stables, make ready gold and silver and all else that you need, and go out into the world. Go in search of the garden of Vleago, and bring me enough fruit from it for me to eat as much as I can three times. Leave as soon as possible, and let a sincere heart bring you back again in a year and a day at the latest."

The next day the three sons took leave of their father and mother, and set out into the wide world. They travelled together a long way, knowing that no one close at hand would be able to tell them where they should look for the garden of Vleago. But when, after a long trek, they came to a place where the road branched three ways, they decided that each of them should take a different road. Finally, they promised that each would stop at that place on his way back, so that they might return to the palace together when the year had passed.

The eldest son turned to the right, for he thought he could see a town in the distance, and he decided he would ask there if anyone knew anything of the garden of Vleago. The middle brother turned to the left, since he could see fields and gardens in the distance. The youngest prince was left the middle road, which led through a long, narrow valley, where he could see nothing either to the left or to the right, or in front of him. So he just rode on and on, until the road brought him to a stream. He went along beside the water, and late in the evening arrived beneath a hill on which he could see a house standing on its own. In front of it stood an enormous giant. The youngest prince greeted him civilly and asked if he might spend the night under his roof.

"Come in, young fellow; I will gladly feed you and give you a bed for the night."

The giant took the prince's horse to the stable, threw a blanket over it, and fed and watered it. Then he bade his guest sit down and eat. There was everything he could wish for on the table: a young lamb, fresh bread and cheese, and the giant even poured wine for the tired prince, not into a horn, but into a cup. The prince was surprised that here in the middle of nowhere the giant had enough of everything to live like a king, but he had no horn from which to drink wine. He drank happily from the cup, ate to his heart's content, and slept like a log until morning.

In the morning the youngest prince made ready for his journey, and asked the giant if he knew where to find the garden of Vleago.

"Vleago? Hm, I have never heard of such a place, and I have travelled the world a good deal. But do not worry — all is not yet lost. By evening you will come to my brother's house. You can spend the night there, and he may know something about Vleago."

The prince thanked the giant kindly, and set off at once. He kept close to the stream, and in the late evening came to a lonely house on a hill again. In front of it stood a huge giant. He, too, made the prince welcome, and fed him well. There was everything on his table, except a knife for the cheese. In the morning the prince asked the giant if he knew where the garden of Vleago might be.

"Vleago? Vleago? Hm, I am old, and I have travelled over much of the world, but I have never heard of Vleago."

The prince hung his head.

"Never you mind, my lad, all is not lost. Just travel on by the stream, and in the evening you will arrive at the house of our eldest brother. He knows the whole world, and besides, the birds of the air and the fish of the waters obey him. If he knows anything of Vleago, he will surely tell you. If he does not, then he will call all the birds and fish, so that they may tell what they know of such a place."

The prince thanked the giant for everything, and went his way. He did not stop until he came to the home of the third of the giants. This time he was not surprised to be generously entertained, only he could not think why there was not so much as a morsel of cheese on such a richly-spread table.

At dawn the prince rose, thanked the giant for everything, and then asked him if he knew anything of the garden of Vleago.

"Hm," said the giant. "I am old, and have travelled the whole world, but never a mention of any Vleago have I heard. But do not hang your head," he added, when he saw how downcast the prince was, "I shall summon all my faithful subjects, the birds and the fish. Perhaps they will know something of Vleago."

He blew on a whistle, and all the fish of the seven seas came swimming along. "Which of you knows something of the garden of Vleago?" he asked.

The fish were silent: not one of them had ever heard of such a place.

"Do not lose heart," the giant comforted the young prince. "I shall send for the birds of the air." He blew two blasts on his whistle, and at once there was such a humming and flapping of wings above their heads that it sounded like a flood-wave rolling down upon them. The giant asked all of them, large and small, if they knew anything of the garden of Vleago. But they shook their heads, saying they knew of no such place.

"Where is the old crow?" asked the giant, sternly. He looked around, and when no one could tell him why the old crow was not in his place, he blew on his whistle a third time. There was a beating of wings like a flock of eagles, and a large crow alighted in the empty space.

"Do you know where the garden of Vleago is?" the giant asked him.

"Indeed I do," replied the crow. "It is far away from here, over many lands and many seas. But I do not know what is in it, for it is guarded by heavily-armed sentries, and nothing on the earth or in the air can escape their shots. Only once every seven years, exactly at noon, the guards fall into a deep sleep. Tomorrow the next seven years will be up."

"Good!" The giant praised his faithful crow. "And now, listen to me. You will take this young man and set him down in front of the garden of Vleago. Until you arrive there, you shall not have a bite to eat, or a drop of water to drink, and you shall not sleep for an instant. Then you will wait there until the young man returns, bring him back, and set him down in front of my house."

The prince thanked the giant and sat on the crow's back as if on a black horse. The bird spread its great black wings and climbed skywards. They flew over many lands and seas, in the glare of the sun and the gentle light of the moon. It was close to midday when the crow finally circled over a magnificent garden.

"We are here," he told the lad. "Hurry, young fellow, if your life is dear to you. Open the gate, run into the garden, take from it what you need, and run back to me. If you do not return quickly, we are both of us lost."

The prince saw sleeping giants and sentries armed to the teeth. They lay on the ground like logs, and snored loudly. Quickly, he ran into the middle of the garden, and picked a full scarf of red apples from a tall tree.

He felt he had never seen such beauty before. His heart leapt with joy, and he ran quickly towards the gate; but suddenly he saw beside the path a house with its door ajar. He pushed it open, and peered inside the hallway. There was a large table there, on which there stood a wine-horn, a cheese-knife, and a large piece of cheese. Thinking that they would be useful to the giants, he wrapped these things up in another scarf, and opened another door. He found himself looking at a large hammock, where a lovely girl was sleeping deeply. The prince dared not even breath when he set his eyes on that unknown beauty. Finally, he wrote a note to say that prince so-and-so had been there, picked a few more apples for his sick father, and took the sleeping girl's golden girdle as a souvenir, and the horn, knife and cheese as presents. He left the note on the table, pushed the girdle under his shirt, and ran back to the crow. He jumped up on the bird's black back, and before long found himself high in the sky.

"Look around!" the crow told him. Down in the garden the sentries and the giants had woken from their deep sleep, and were shouting, hitting and slashing at one another, angry that some thief had escaped with red apples from the most beautiful of the apple trees.

The crow flew higher still; he crossed many seas and many lands, without resting or taking refreshment before he alighted in front of the house of the lord of the birds and fish. The prince slept there once more, and in the morning he left the large piece of cheese on the giant's table. Once more he thanked the giant for everything, then jumped onto his horse, now rested, and quickly flew off. Before evening he reached the home of the middle giant. The prince was glad to take refreshment and to rest till morning. When the sun rose over the deep valley, the young man placed the knife beside the piece of cheese, mounted his horse, and was gone. At the house of the third giant he left the large wine-horn, and hurried on to the place where he had taken leave of his brothers.

Exhausted, he arrived at the head of the deep valley, but his brothers were nowhere to be seen. So he tied his mount to a tree, lay down in the grass with the scarf full of apples under his head, and went to sleep. Before long the two elder brothers arrived, but the youngest slept on soundly. He did not even feel them take the scarf from under his head.

"Whew!" cried both at once. "These apples are indeed different from ours!"

They were angry that their brother had outdone them.

"Now father will favour him even more than before," snapped the eldest bitterly. "You'll see how our baby brother will have them all at his feet, and we shall be pushed aside."

The middle brother felt the same, so they agreed to divide the red apples equally between them, and to fill their brother's scarf with the humble apples they had managed to gather. In a brace of shakes it was done. Then they woke their brother up, and set off homewards together.

The moment they got home, the eldest prince went to his father and presented him with a scarf full of red apples. As soon as the old king took his first bite, his strength began to return. When he ate the apples from the middle son's scarf, all his old strength and health came back to him.

"Have you, too, brought me apples?" he asked the youngest son.

"I have indeed, father," the youngest prince assured him, and untied his scarf. All gasped as a pile of rough green apples rolled out.

"Fie! What is this you have brought?" the eldest brother rebuked the youngest. "Such fruit would kill our father. If we put it in the pigs' trough, I imagine they will die, too." And at once he called a servant, and ordered him to tip the apples in the pigs' trough.

In a little while a wild shouting was heard from the yard below. The pigs had eaten the apples, rolled over on their backs, and given up the ghost.

The king had never been so angry in his life. Without hesitation, he summoned the captain of the guard, and ordered him to take the youngest prince into the forest and make an end of him.

The captain of the guard was taken aback by the order; he liked the youngest prince a great deal, and begged the king at least to wait till morning, saying that wrath is a poor counsellor, and that no one could be sure just how it had been with the apples.

"If you do not obey me this instant, it will be the worse for you!" the king shouted at the captain.

"May you not live to regret it dearly!" said the captain, boldly.

But in the end, with a heavy heart, he set off into the forest to lead the youngest prince on his last journey.

"I am not afraid of death," said the prince, sadly. "I look it in the face with courage. But it grieves me that my father and all those dearest to me consider me a knave. And the truth is indeed that I picked my father a full scarf of the reddest apples in the garden of

Vleago, and returned home with them. I do not know who put those terrible green apples in my scarf, but I swear that what I have told you is the truth."

At that moment a wild boar came tearing out of the thicket and charged at the captain of the guard. It was just about to pierce him with its horns, when the prince leapt to his aid.

"Thank you for saving my life," the man said to the prince, when he had recovered from the shock. "I believe you to be telling the truth, and I shall spare your life, if you do as I tell you. Hide far away, in the densest part of the forest, and show yourself to no one. Take off your shirt; I shall stain it with the blood of the boar, and take it to the king. Do not despair: I daresay all will turn out for the best."

The next morning the captain of the guard went before the king and gave him his son's shirt.

"I am afraid that you have wronged your youngest son, and that you will regret it bitterly!"

"You have nothing to fear, for it is not your concern!" the king snapped back.

A year and a day passed from the moment the youngest prince had entered the garden of Vleago. It was then that the spell on the sleeping queen was broken. She had been cursed long ago by a powerful wizard, who declared that she must lie there as if she were dead until she was found by a prince whom the guards that watched the garden day and night would not overcome. But it was to take another whole year and a day for her to wake up from her deep sleep. Only then would the power of the spell be broken, only then would she again be free.

When the queen awoke and read the note on the table, she resolved at once to go to Ireland to find her deliverer. On the way she called upon her three brothers, the giants, to release them, too, from the spell. The moment she arrived and touched them, they changed back into the selfsame young princes they had been when the wizard had placed a spell on them.

They wept with joy and embraced each other happily. But there was no time for rejoicing. Their sister urged them to hurry.

"We must go at once to the kingdom of Ireland to find the prince who came to the garden of Vleago in search of apples, and who set us all free. I had a dream that evil had befallen him. Now he may need our help."

The queen and her three brothers mounted swift horses, and sped at the head of a great company towards the kingdom of Ireland. They brought many rich gifts for the Irish king. Bowing before him, the eldest of the foreign princes spoke on behalf of the others:

"King of Ireland, your son entered the garden of Vleago in search of apples, and delivered all four of us and our country from an evil spell. We have come to thank him."

The king called his eldest son, who said at once that it was he who had brought the apples from the garden of Vleago.

"Thank you, dear prince," said the queen, with a smile. "Now tell us all that you saw there."

The prince knew that the game was up, but he lied and told tales till the heavens cracked. At each of his false words the queen frowned more darkly. In a while she interrupted him: "Begone from my sight, you liar! You are not even fit to pasture sheep, like your father!"

The eldest prince left in disgrace, and then the middle son came and quickly made up a story of what he had seen in the garden of Vleago. But the queen did not allow him to prattle for long.

"Begone from my sight!" she interrupted him. "You liar, you are not even fit to herd swine, like your father!"

The King of Ireland was so ashamed he wished the ground might swallow him up. Suddenly, he did not know what to make of it all. But just then the queen turned to him: "If the deliverer of Vleago does not come to me in three days, our army will overrun Ireland and burn it to the ground for the nest of liars it is, and will kill all the menfolk. There are enough of us to pour over your land like the sea in flood."

The poor king did not know what to do, and news of the danger which threatened spread like wildfire. The captain of the guard heard of all that had occurred, and he went before the king.

[103] "Sire, did I not tell you that you had wronged your youngest son,

and that you would regret it bitterly? But now there is no time for remorse. Luckily for you and for all of us, I did not obey your order, being convinced that it was unjust. I did not slay your son, for he saved my own life. He is hiding in the thickest part of the forest, far from the royal castle, but I daresay I can bring him here in three days."

"Go! Go with all speed!" groaned the Irish king.

In two days the captain of the guard found the youngest prince in the densest part of the forest, far from his father's castle. He brought him home by the shortest route, and when the servants had bathed the prince and dressed him in his finest clothes, on the third day he went before the queen from the garden of Vleago.

"Was it really you who picked the apples from the garden of Vleago?" she asked him, smiling.

"Forgive me, I was indeed there. I needed the apples greatly for my sick father."

"Very well," said the queen. "You did well to go there. Now tell me what you saw and did there."

The youngest prince told the whole story from the beginning: how he journeyed through the long, narrow valley, how the three giants gave him a bed for the night and fed him well, how the third giant called the crow and how the bird had taken him right to the garden of Vleago. And he told of the misfortune which had overtaken him when his scarf turned out to be full of sour green apples which killed the pigs.

"But I still have a souvenir from the garden of Vleago," he concluded at last, and took out the queen's golden girdle.

"It is mine, mine!" cried the queen in happiness, and she did not know how to thank her deliverer enough. Then the three princes came forward and thanked him warmly for setting them free.

"You will not recognize us in this form," said the eldest. "We were enchanted as giants, and we helped you when we saw that you were a man with a good heart. You said nothing of the fact that you had no horn, knife or cheese at supper, but in the garden of Vleago you remembered us."

"And now come," said the queen. "We shall go together to your father, and tell him that his kingdom is no longer in danger, for you are our deliverer. And when your mother kisses you, ask her to take this ring which I give you. When she takes it, order the ring to squeeze her finger until she reveals who your brothers are. Have no fear, she will not harm you, and you will bring to light the truth."

The prince did as he was told, and when his mother slipped the ring on her finger, he called out, "Ring, squeeze my mother's finger until she tells who my brothers are!"

The queen burst into a flood of bitter tears, and unwillingly told the king the story of what had happened long ago.

"Husband, forgive me what I did in misfortune, for I did it only to spare you grief. You recall that when our first son was born, you were at war in a far-off country. A son was born to us, but on the third day he died. I was half mad with grief. Then I thought how I might save you at least from such sorrow. I knew that a sturdy boy-child had been born to the wife of our shepherd the day before mine. I sent a faithful servant to persuade her with gold and silver and fine words to give me her son and to bury mine as her own. At first she would not hear of it, but then she thought how it would be better for her boy to grow up in the royal castle as a king's son than in a shepherd's cottage, and in the end she gave the child to my servant. So the shepherd's son lived like a prince. Two years later a second son was born, but he, too, died. That very night I exchanged the dead boy for a live one. The swineherd's wife had a son at the same time as I, but hers was healthy and strong. So the swineherd's son, too, lived in the royal castle like a prince. Two years later I gave birth to a third son, our youngest child. He was the only one who lived, and I swear to you that he is your son and mine."

The king would rather have been six feet under the ground at that moment than in the royal chamber. Beside himself with rage, he leapt up and drew his sword. Only the words of his son held his hand:

"Father, do not punish the innocent with the guilty, without passing judgement."

"Very well," cried the king. "Then hear my judgement. These two false rogues shall be horsewhipped out of my land. If they ever return, I shall have them torn apart by wild boars. And you, guards, take the queen and throw her in prison. Build a great fire at the stake, and at dawn you shall burn her. Let the queen pay for all the suffering, shame and grief she has caused by her deception."

"No, father," the prince spoke up again. "For she is my own good mother. Forgive her for deceiving you: she did so to spare you great grief. And she has already paid for her guilt a hundred times over in sorrow. Forget the evil, now that all has turned out well."

By and by the king's heart softened when he saw what a good, courageous and powerful king his son would make.

Then they all rejoiced. The Irish prince married the delivered queen of Vleago, and her brothers, too, found lovely brides, and all have lived happily since then, if they have not yet died.

Glen Gowan

Many years ago a terrible drought came, and the sun baked the earth throughout the land. The meadows and hills turned as brown as old leather; the moment a breeze got up, clouds of dust rose from the earth as when a row of waggons passes along the road. All the greenery had long since withered; folks wrung their hands in despair, animals dropped with hunger and thirst, and even in the streams and springs only a few last drops of water remained.

For a whole two months there was not a drop of rain to refresh the parched earth. Fine cows and sheep died in their hundreds; many a farmer met his ruin, and was left with only a beggar's stick.

The elves tried to help good folk as best they could, letting them drive their cattle into their own meadows and woodland glades, but it was not enough. No wonder, for it took no more than half a day for the ravenous cows and sheep to strip the lush greenery, where the elves were wont to tarry from spring till late autumn. Then the elves went underground and wrung their hands just like the people of the villages.

"Whatever will become of us," they lamented. "Good green grass will not grow on such a wasteland in a whole year." And they decided that now, in their greatest need, those who most deserved their help were those who had not only never harmed them, but had always held them in respect, and more than once lent them a hand when they needed it.

The man most beloved of the elves was farmer Sandy. He had the kindest of hearts, and even when he had only a farthing to his name himself, he did all that was in his power to help others. No pauper ever left his cottage empty-handed or without a full stomach.

In the end poverty overtook Sandy, too, when one day his two cows, the family's livelihood, both died.

Sandy's wife and children wept bitterly, and in the end fell asleep. But the farmer did not sleep a wink. From dusk to midnight he sat by the hearth, gazing at the dying embers and pondering how he might save his family from starvation. Suddenly he sat bolt upright, as he heard a loud noise.

"What is it? Who is it?" he muttered. Then all of a sudden a heavy purse fell down the chimney and thudded to the floor. Sandy opened it, and saw a pile of gold pieces with a piece of paper folded on top. He opened it and read: "A favour for a favour! Take the sovereigns and buy some cows!"

Sandy did not know whether to believe his good fortune, wondering if his troubles had not taken away his reason. Before daybreak he left the house, crossed the hills to Kinross, and bought two fine cows from a rich landowner. But when he got home, his head again began to ache with bewilderment: how was he to feed and water the animals?

Sandy's wife and children jumped with joy, and tended the cows like honoured guests. They cleaned out the cowshed, scrubbed the manger, brought what was left of the hay, and gave them the water set aside for the whole family. They said to themselves, "Better for us to go thirsty than for our cows to die again."

The farmer, meanwhile, was roaming the meadows and hills in search of a patch of green grass to take the cows to. All of a sudden he heard a voice coming from beneath the gorse: "Drive the cows into Glen Gowan!"

The farmer shook his head in disbelief, and the voice came again:

"Why suffer for nought; drive the cows into Glen Gowan this very day!"

The farmer wondered greatly, since everyone in those parts knew that only thistles, burdock and the odd thorn bush grew in Glen Gowan: poor fare even for a goat, let alone a couple of cows! Sandy could almost have laughed at such advice, but he was afraid he might offend the elves who had helped him. So he went back home with his head hung low, took the cows, and led them to the place where the elves had told him to pasture them.

"They have had enough hay and water today," he said to himself. "No matter if I find nothing; maybe tomorrow I shall think of something better."

He went down into the glen, and suddenly stood stock still, as if his feet had sunk into the ground. He rubbed his eyes, then whooped with joy like a small boy, for there was not a thistle or a weed in sight. It seemed to him as if someone had carefully weeded the whole of Glen Gowan. The bottom of the hollow was carpeted with thick green grass, and down the slopes ran a stream of crystal-clear water.

He set the cows to graze, drank from the spring, and lay down to rest in the grass, happy and contented.

There was good grazing waiting for Sandy's cows the next day, and the next. Every morning Glen Gowan was as fresh as if it had rained in the night. The cows gave so much milk that the farmer's wife filled all their buckets and pails every day. The whole family had milk to drink, even the neighbours' children could drink their fill, until it was a wonder they did not burst. And there was still enough left to make butter and curds. The butter from Sandy's farm was so good that the gentlemen in the town soon wanted no other.

In time the neighbours began to envy Sandy, though he had always helped them, and they had never given him so much as a tuft of grass. They came to see him, but not as good neighbours: rather as enemies.

"Sandy, we are oppressed by poverty, ground under the heel of misfortune in this drought, and here you are living like a gentleman, piling gold upon gold. But mark our words — tomorrow we, too, will take our cows to graze in Glen Gowan!"

The farmer looked from one to the other. "Have some sense, laddies: there's scarcely enough grass for two cows there," he said to them quietly.

But the neighbours would not listen, and the next morning they all drove their cows down to Glen Gowan. All at once there were as many cows there as at the county fair. But the wonder of it was that while Sandy's cows grazed there contentedly as always, the rest of them were unable to tear up a single blade of grass, or drink a single drop of water — as if their necks had turned quite stiff. When their

owners took them home to milk them, not a drop of milk dripped into their pails.

Luckily, that night a tremendous storm put an end to the long drought, and after two months rain soaked the earth. Slowly the countryside became green again; people came to life, and as they got back their work, they got back their reason, too, and soon made up their quarrel with kind-hearted Sandy.

Sandy lived better day by day, and when he grew old he looked after his whole family well, and not only the neighbours, but folk for miles around sought his advice on many things. And Glen Gowan was full of fresh green grass even in years of drought.

The Truthful Prince

Long, long ago, a powerful king reigned in Galicia. During his reign the land enjoyed peace: the tradesmen went about their trades, the merchants bought and sold their merchandise, and the soldiers watched over the country's borders. All in all the king might have been happy, had he not been afflicted with one great grief. He would often walk in the forests alone, trying to forget his sorrow. But when he saw the birds flying to their nests to feed their young ones, a mother bear playing with her cubs, or a mare and her foal running about the forest glade, again he would begin to worry over what would become of the kingdom when he was gone, for he had no heir. No wonder that, at just such a moment, he forgot to look where he was going, and got lost in the forest. Tired and weary, he came to a spring above a thicket, and sighed with relief.

"At least I can have a drink and take a rest; then I will be able to think more clearly how I am to get out of the forest," he said to himself.

But the spring was covered in fallen leaves and clogged with mud, and the water was only just able to trickle out from the rocks. The king bent down, gathered up the leaves, and laid them beneath a stone some distance away, so that they might not be blown about by the wind. Then he cleaned out the spring, mended the stone channel along which the water flowed, and lay down in the grass to rest from his labours.

No sooner had he closed his eyes than, from behind the nearest of the trees, he heard a thin little voice say, "Thank you, my dear king, for helping us to clean the spring. We will gladly grant you a wish in return; tell us what you most desire."

The king started in amazement — then he caught sight of a water nymph leaning on an oak tree. She was smiling at him, her green eyes twinkling like bright stars.

"It was nothing," sighed the king. "I am always happy to be of service to you, guardians of the waters. And if you have recognized me even in this smock, then you will know that I desire nothing more than to have an heir to my throne."

"Have no fear on that account," replied the nymph. "You shall welcome the summer with a son in your arms," she promised, and vanished in a gust of wind.

When high summer came, and the sun seared the land, honoured guests came from miles around to greet the king's first-born son in the royal castle. The queen herself handed the boy to his father; then they both wept with joy, as they smiled at their son.

That evening, when the guests had gathered around the table and the queen was sleeping peacefully, three nymphs from the forest spring came and stood beside the golden cradle.

"What gifts shall we bestow upon him?" they asked one another over the head of the sleeping child.

"We have already granted him beauty; now we shall add to it good health and sound sense," they decided. But after a moment the oldest of the fairies added, "Lest he become proud, if he is beautiful, healthy and clever, let ass's ears mar his beauty a little."

And so it was to be. The prince grew, and grew; he was healthy, and there was not a sharper lad in the whole of the kingdom, or in the neighbouring ones. The only thing which troubled his parents was that the lad's ears grew longer day by day, and were just like those of an ass. At last the old king resolved that he would allow only his most trusted valet to attend the prince; that he would not only dress his hair, but also cut it, and that every day he should put a broad golden coronet on the boy's head to cover up his ears. No one but the royal parents and the valet was allowed anywhere near the prince's head. The valet was paid a royal ransom, but the king threatened him sternly:

"If you should ever once mention the prince's ears to anyone in the world, you shall go to the executioner! You could not hide from me, even if you were to fly behind the clouds; if you betray the royal secret, you are death's vassal."

[113] For many years the valet kept the king's secret stoutly. Bags of

money were dearer to him than idle gossip. So, day in, day out, he cared for the prince like his own son.

When the prince grew to be a young man, there was none, at home or abroad, who did not praise his wisdom and skill, kindness and beauty. More than once the valet grimaced secretly when he heard pretty young girls chattering about how handsome the young prince was, as pretty as a picture. If they knew what I know, then they would speak differently, he thought to himself.

And so it was that, as time went by, the prince's secret began to lie heavy on the valet's mind. He started to worry that one day he might cry out in his sleep, so loud that the castle walls would shake, "The prince has ass's ears!"

One day the valet went for a walk alone in the royal gardens, trying to think of a way to relieve himself of his burden and rid himself of the peril he was in. He was walking beside a stream, and he left the garden and walked on and on. By and by he came to a quiet creek where reeds grew among the willow trees. There was no living creature in sight, only the sound of birds twittering in the distance. The valet lay down on the ground and fell into a deep sleep. He had a strange dream: a beautiful young maiden came up to him, bent down and whispered in his ear, "Make a hole in the soft earth here; whisper your secret into it, fill in the hole and plant a clump of grass there. Then your words will remain under the earth. No one will hear them, and the earth will not betray your secret!"

The valet leapt up joyfully, and in a moment he had whispered three times into a hole by the stream, "Our prince has ass's ears! Our prince has ass's ears! Our prince has ass's ears!"

At that instant it was as if a millstone had been untied from the valet's neck. He filled in the hole, planted a clump of grass there, and, whistling to himself, set off home.

By some misfortune there was a young reed among the grass. It grew quickly and became strong, and when some shepherds passed by the stream with their flocks they cut the reed and made whistles from it. That evening they tuned them up, and in the morning when they set off with their sheep, they blew on them. But what a terrible thing! The whistles piped in harmony, "Our prince has ass's ears!" [114]

The shepherds did not know what to make of such strange whistling, so they pushed their whistles into the sleeves of their tunics. But the story of the shepherds' song spread swiftly through the countryside. Before long the king himself heard it. Without hesitation he gave his guards the order:

"Bring me the shepherds with their pipes, and the prince's valet with the executioner!"

Before the shepherds knew what was happening, they were standing before the king.

"Play me the tune you played this morning!"

The shepherds were trembling like aspen leaves, but there was nothing for it but to take out their whistles from their sleeves and play them. The moment they blew on them, three voices echoed through the castle hall, "Our prince has ass's ears!"

The valet half swooned with terror, and swore that he had not told the secret to a living soul in the whole world.

The king, beside himself with anger, would not even allow the valet to finish speaking.

"Take away this base deceiver, and perform your duty!" he shouted to the executioner.

Just then the prince came forward, took the golden coronet from his head, revealing his ears, and knelt before the king.

"No, good father; I beg you, no!" he cried. "On my knees I beg you: forgive me for going against your will, but you must not punish anyone for speaking the truth. What of it that I have an ass's ears? At least they remind me that I am not to say or do anything stupid, or behave like a stubborn ass!"

No one in the royal hall could take his eyes off the prince. Thus it was that no one noticed that the oldest water nymph had crept in. Now she spoke with a voice like clear water splashing in a spring, "You have done well, my prince, to defend the truth even in the face of your father's anger. You are bold and wise, and without pride, so there is no need for you to be burdened with ass's ears any more."

And as soon as the prince shook his head a little, he had ears just like anyone else's.

What rejoicing there was throughout the land! The king at once handed his own golden crown over to his son, and invited guests from nine kingdoms to a feast. All made merry there, young and old, valet and shepherds, lords and servant-girls, and most of all the old king and queen and their only son, together with the most beautiful princess from the ninth kingdom. Along with the other guests the oldest minstrel at the king's court joined in the merrymaking. At once he composed a long ballad about all that had happened, and taught the younger ones to sing it, so that people throughout the land might know what a great king they had.

Liam Donn

There was once a mighty king of Ireland who had twelve sons. Not even the king himself or his queen could tell which of them was the wisest, the best, the cleverest; nor was there any need, for the boys lived together in harmony, helping each other and learning only good from one another.

One day the king went to a wise old man for advice, and in the end the seer told him:

"My liege, good fortune will leave your house if you do not send one of your sons out into the world. Order him not to return until he has undertaken such a task as none before him has ever dared. Let him not come home until he has earned the wonder and admiration of the world!"

"What is this you are saying, old man?" cried the startled king. "I daresay every young man should go out into the world to learn its ways. But am I to close my door to one of my sons, and forbid him to return until he has performed some deed such as no other has ever dared? It would be sending my own son to certain death."

"Remember, my liege, that otherwise good fortune will turn its back on you," the old sage repeated. And since the Irish king had great faith in his counsellor, he resolved with a heavy heart that he must take his advice. He returned to his castle and told his wife they must decide which of their sons to send from their home. The queen burst into tears, and did not know what to do for the best. In the end they determined to resolve the matter by the hand of fate. Whichever of their sons was the last to return from hunting that day should be sent out into the world to perform a deed which no other had ever dared.

The king and queen stood at the gate as the young princes returned from their hunting. The youngest of them remained some distance behind the rest, and was the last to come in. The queen's heart nearly broke. She loved all her sons, but the youngest, Liam Donn, was the dearest of all to her. The king, too, was reluctant to close the gate on his youngest son.

"Let us wait until tomorow," he said with a sigh.

But the next day the youngest son tarried even longer, and his brothers had long been home when Liam approached the gate of his father's castle.

"Wait one more day," the queen begged her husband, and once again the king did not shut the gate on him.

But when Liam Donn returned after the others on the third day, too, the king had no choice but to keep to his word and to close the gate on the last of his sons.

"My son," said the king, "I see that fate has decided that you should go out into the world at once. This gate shall be open to you only when you have done a deed so bold that none before you has ever had the courage to do it. Come home when you have earned the wonder and admiration of the world. I should rather die than banish you thus, but I have no choice in the matter."

"Have no fear for me," the prince replied. "I shall not be a poor vagabond. You yourself, father, have always taught us that we are never to eat our bread or blow on our porridge without earning them. Only tell me what task I am to perform."

"Very well, my son; your words please me. Listen: I shall set you a task. My friend, the King of Greece, has twelve daughters, just as I have twelve sons. The youngest of them, Una the White-Handed, is lost, and he will lose her forever if no one saves her. Go, Liam Donn; go and rescue her. Return only when you have found her and delivered her."

"I shall go at once, but first I must take my leave of my mother and my brothers. When my mother has given me her blessing, I shall set off into the world." With these words Liam Donn took a run and leaped over the walls of his father's castle. He sat down on a stool before the hearth, and sighed deeply. At that moment the beams of the ceiling gave a loud crack, and the steel stool sank deep into the stone floor in front of the hearth.

"It is sad for me that we must thus be parted, my son," said the king, "for I see that you will be a fine figure of a man."

In the meantime, his mother mixed the dough for three loaves of bread. Into the first she mixed a little mother's milk, into the second mead, and to the third she added a few drops of blood.

"Liam," she said, "I send you on your journey with a mother's blessing and three loaves of bread. All my strength is baked into them. Any man you strike with one of my loaves will fall down dead at once."

The youngest prince thanked his mother, said farewell to his father and his brothers, and strode off into the wide world in search of Una the White-Handed.

He rode, and rode, from dawn till dusk, until at last he spotted a single light shining far off in a deep valley. It led him to a house in which he found a girl as pretty as a picture. She had a golden star on her forehead, and was combing her hair with a golden comb. She started when she caught sight of the stranger in the doorway.

Liam Donn greeted her civilly, and asked if he might spend the night there.

"Run for your life, young sir," cried the girl. "The terrible giant will soon return home, and if he finds you here he is certain to tear you to little pieces."

"Indeed I shall not run away from him," replied Liam Donn, "nor shall I let him tear me to pieces."

At that moment the giant returned.

"Fie, fie!" he roared, until Liam Donn was nearly deafened. "I smell a thieving Irishman! Ah, there you are! Let me see, too big for one bite, too small for two. Now, am I to drop you in the cauldron, or grind you to dust like a pinch of snuff?"

"The devil take you, you oaf!" retorted Liam Donn. "Why don't you try your strength with me, instead of your boasting!"

They clenched fiercely, pitting their strength against each other. They wrestled for a long time; sometimes it seemed that the giant would pin the prince to the floor, sometimes the big fellow lay helpless on his back. But Liam Donn would certainly have come off the worse in the end, had he not remembered his mother's loaves. With his last ounce of strength he pulled one out and struck the giant with it as hard as he could. The giant fell over like a bale of hay, but just managed to take a bite of the bread. He opened his eyes a little, and said in a kind voice, "Welcome, son of my only sister; welcome to my house. I recognized who you were when I tasted the bread. No one in the world can bake bread such as that except your mother. I will help you all I can, if you will only place the bread on my wound."

Liam Donn did not know whether to believe his ears, but he did as he was bidden, and pressed the loaf against the giant's chest. At that instant the giant changed into a handsome man, who leaped to his feet and embraced Liam Donn. In no time at all they were sitting at a richly-spread table, and the lad's uncle was explaining how he had lived for many years in solitude as a giant, and that only the son of his only sister could release him from the spell by overcoming him in combat.

"Liam, tell me how I may help you in return," his uncle begged him.

"Only good advice can help me," Liam Donn told him. "I wish to [120]

know where Una the White-Handed, daughter of the Greek king, is to be found."

"I cannot tell you that, for I know nothing of her. But perhaps our middle brother can help you. It will be easy enough for you to find him. Here you have a red bridle. When you shake it a red pony will come running from the stables and take you straight to the house of my middle brother. If you overcome him, he too will be released, and will help you."

Liam Donn thanked his uncle, and by evening the red pony had taken him right up to a solitary house. There he defeated his second uncle in combat, returning to him his human form. But the middle brother sent him on to the youngest, for he knew nothing of Una the White-Handed.

Just as the evening mists were settling on the valley, Liam Donn arrived before the house of the youngest giant. There, too, he found a beautiful woman with a golden star on her brow and a golden comb in her hand. She was most startled when she saw the young man in the doorway.

"Run for your life!" she cried, by way of greeting. "The terrible giant will soon be home, and if he finds you here, who knows what fiendish death awaits you!"

"I have never learnt to run from giants, or from goblins, let alone from men. I daresay he will not harm me."

"See, he is leaping across the hills, and crossing two valleys at a single stride!" cried the woman, wringing her hands.

At that moment the giant arrived home, panting.

"Fie, fie!" he called out, so loudly it was a wonder the stone walls did not come crashing down. "I smell a thieving Irishman! Ah, there you are! I see you are too much for one gulp, too little for two. I am not quite sure whether to take one puff and blow you into the Eastern World, or to take two and blow you into the Western!"

When Liam Donn saw the five-headed giant, he was a little taken aback, but he did not let it show.

"May all the devils in hell take you, you oaf!" he retorted. "Instead of boasting, try your strength with me!"

They threw themselves at each other like a pair of wild boars. In [122] the place where they stood and fought, they trampled the floor to stone, and wherever they fell, they left a hole it would have taken a cartload of sand to fill.

When they had been fighting for a long time, Liam Donn was seized with a fit of anger. He caught hold of the giant and drove him into the grey stone up to his knees. The giant jumped out, but this time Liam Donn drove him in up to his waist. But still the giant got out. Then Liam Donn summoned all his strength and thrust the giant in up to his eyes.

"If I have ever obeyed my mother, then I do so now!" cried Liam Donn, and, taking the last of his mother's loaves, brought it crashing down on the giant's head. But the giant took a bite out of it, and calmed down at once.

"Welcome, son of my only sister; welcome to my house!" cried the giant. "Spare my life, and press the loaf to my head. I will help you in any way I can."

Thus Liam Donn returned the third of his mother's brothers to his human form. With what joy it was that his uncle and his wife heard how he had delivered the other two of his uncles!

"Tell me, Liam, how can I help you?" asked his uncle.

"By telling me where I can find Una the White-Handed, daughter of the King of Greece, and what danger threatens her. My father ordered me to release her; until I do so I may not return home."

"There is nothing simpler than to tell you where to find Una. But it will be a more difficult matter to save her and you from peril. Stay here till morning, then I shall prepare you for your journey. It will not be easy, I can tell you, for if you are to set free Una the White-Handed you must overcome a fearsome dragon."

Then Liam Donn and his uncle ate, drank, and told tales and adventures of the renowned hero Finn, so that the night passed quickly. Finally, they took strength from a deep sleep.

When day dawned, Liam Donn leapt straight out of bed, ate a good breakfast, and buckled on a sword of tempered steel.

"Now I shall give you a bridle, and my horse will take you straight to the banks of the deep river where Una the White-Handed sits," his uncle told him. "All those around her are weeping and wailing, for the time is nigh for the terrible dragon to come out of the sea and carry her off, heaven knows where to. Good people accompanied her to the river, but no one can help her now if you do not save her."

Liam Donn thanked his uncle, and began to say farewell.

"Wait," his uncle told him, "you do not yet know what awaits you. You will come across three hills: one of steel, one of fire and one of werewolves. Take this healing ointment, and keep it safe. If you prick yourself, burn yourself, or are poisoned, you have only to rub it on the wound, and it will be healed at once."

The moment Liam Donn shook his uncle's bridle in front of the house, a grey horse came running along, and as soon as his rider had leapt upon his back, he made straight for the river where Una the White-Handed sat. The horse sped along, its hooves not even touching the ground, and before long they arrived at a hill of steel, thickly set with long needles. Liam's steed gathered speed, leapt into the air like a winged stallion, and flew high over the hill of steel. Neither Liam nor his mount was pricked by the needles, and they thundered on without resting. They saw the hill of fire from afar, for its flames rose high into the sky.

"Jump, my faithful steed!" Liam Donn urged the horse, and the creature flew high above the hill, leaving it far behind them at a single leap. Neither horse nor rider was harmed by the flames. Now only one obstacle lay in their path, but that was the most fearsome of all: the hill of werewolves. On it lived thousands of venomous werewolves, whose tiniest bite brought death to all living creatures.

The horse took a good run, and with a great leap rose high above the hill, and began slowly to descend. But the werewolves, too, jumped into the air, howling and screeching and spraying venom all about them. One of them managed to sink its venomous fangs into the horse's leg. The poor creature neighed desperately, and would surely have breathed its last very shortly, if Liam Donn had not had the healing ointment his uncle gave him.

"Have no fear, faithful steed," he told the horse, rubbing the ointment on the wound. It was so effective that from that very moment the horse was able to gallop again at full speed. In a while they

stopped to refresh themselves with food and water. Liam Donn brushed the horse down to get rid of any traces of poison, and took off his heavy boots, which the werewolves had spat upon. Putting on a pair of deerskin shoes, he swung into the saddle, and they sped off again.

It was not long before they were able to see the gleam of a broad river in the distance. A tall, bare, cliff-face rose from its banks, and it was there that Una the White-Handed was fettered to a rock with heavy iron chains.

Beneath the rock stood a crowd of people, all weeping so profusely that the ground was unable to soak up their tears. But there was no one who dared disobey the monster's orders, which were that as soon as the sun climbed to the top of the heavens at noon, they were to chain Una the White-Handed to the cliff beside the river, and leave her alone. It was from there the creature was to come.

With one bound the horse was across the broad river, as if it were no more than a mere brook. Before its hooves touched the ground, Liam Donn called out, "Good folk, why are you weeping so sorely that the earth cannot soak up your tears? And you, fair maiden, why do you lament so that even the stones must take pity on you?"

"The stones, perhaps, but the monster, never. That is why I am lamenting, for I am chained to the rock so he can take me. He has threatened to lay waste the whole country if he does not get Una the White-Handed."

"Have no fear, Una," said Liam Donn. "I shall not let the monster take you; I shall fight with him, and deliver both you and the country from doom. Indeed, that is why I have come half way across the world from Ireland."

Many of those present took heart at these words, but Una the White-Handed scarcely heard them. She shook her head, replying quietly, "Thank you, bold sir; but all is in vain, for there is no one on earth who can overcome the monster. He has already slain without mercy many a brave warrior, and soon I am fated to meet the same end. You at least can still save yourself."

At that the waters parted, and a vile three-headed creature came towards them. It lashed the water until tall waves washed the shore. [126]

Soon the monster raised itself from the water and stepped out onto the bank.

"Harken to me, hideous one," shouted Liam. "Keep your claws off what doesn't belong to you!" And he charged towards the beast, his steel sword drawn. But the sea-dragon fought fiercely. They chopped and slashed till evening, but late in the afternoon Liam Donn managed to cut off one of the creature's three heads.

The beast plunged into the water, roaring out, "Tomorrow I shall be back, and woe upon this whole country if I do not find Una the White-Handed chained to the rock!"

"If you return tomorrow, you will lose another of your heads!" Liam Donn called after it.

Early the next morning Liam Donn was waiting for the beast by the river-bank. And again the waters parted and the monster dragged itself out of the river. Liam drew his sword, and once more they chopped and slashed until the sun sank in the west. When Liam Donn saw that evening was approaching and the fearsome creature was still alive, his heart fell, and in despair he swung more resolutely than ever at the dragon, until another of its heads rolled to the ground. The monster roared horribly, and plunged into the water like a stone.

"Tomorrow I shall return, and tear you to pieces!" it threatened. "Woe betide this country if I do not find Una the White-Handed chained to the rocks."

On the morning of the third day, Liam Donn was again waiting by the waterside for the monster to appear. More dead than alive, Una the White-Handed pressed herself against the rocks. She no longer feared for herself, had no thought for the cruel death which might await her, but was afraid for the life of the bold Irish youth.

The news had spread throughout the land that an unknown hero had fought with the dragon for two days, and had cut off two of its heads. Now there were so many people gathered on the river bank that the whole of the shore was darkened with their host. All wished to see the valiant young warrior fight against the monster.

They did not have long to wait before the waters parted once again. The terrible creature came towards them. It climbed onto the bank, and roared fit to crack the cliff face when it saw Liam standing there, sword in hand. It turned, and thrashed, and struck out, and parried Liam's blows.

The sun was low in the western sky, and Liam Donn saw that the dragon was still alive. So he gripped his sword more firmly than ever, swung it with new fury — and the last of the monster's heads went rolling into the river.

The crowd on the bank roared with exultation, people embraced one another, whooped and sang and danced, and celebrated the delivery of Una the White-Handed. Many of them scrambled down to the waterside, broke open the chains, and carried Una up the bank. And then, what a welcoming, and hugging, and embracing there was, and laughter and weeping till the sound of it reached the skies!

Liam Donn, too, tried to push his way through the crowd to Una the White-Handed. Now he saw her, now she was lost from sight in the crowd. Then he caught sight of her again, smiling at him sweetly. Just as she stretched out her hands towards him, there was a loud calling of:

"Make way! Make way for the King of Greece!"

At that moment the crowd tore Liam Donn apart from Una the White-Handed, and in the pell-mell someone even dragged one of his shoes from his foot. All wished to see the king press his rescued daughter to his breast. Just then they had all forgotten about Liam Donn. He slipped quietly from among the inquisitive onlookers, and slowly walked away. As the evening mist gathered by the riverside, he came to a lonely cottage and asked for a bed for the night. They received him gratefully, and sat him down at the table at once.

In the meantime the princess had been accompanied to the royal castle by crowds of rejoicing subjects; a great celebration was held, with music and dancing, and a fabulous feast. The king and his daughter searched among the guests for their deliverer, but he was nowhere to be found, either at the tables, or on the dance-floor, or anywhere else. It was as if the bold young man had been swallowed up in the bowels of the earth; all they could find was one of his deerskin shoes.

"Father dear," begged the princess, "if you wish me to be happy and gay, have them find the one whose foot this shoe fits."

The shoe did the rounds of the gentlemen and soldiers, and more than one of them secretly sacrificed a piece of his big toe or his heel. But all to no avail — the deerskin shoe gave them all away.

Towards dawn the king's soldiers arrived at the cottage where Liam Donn was spending the night, for they had orders to search the countryside all around for the young man whose foot the shoe fitted. Half asleep, he put out his foot — and the shoe fitted like a glove. As soon as Liam Donn had rubbed the sleep from his eyes, they quickly took him to the royal palace, as the king had ordered.

There was great rejoicing at the king's court when Liam Donn arrived. The king himself came out to meet him, and embraced him like his own son. He did not know how to thank him.

"I, too, wish to thank you, my deliverer," Una the White-Handed greeted him, and she smiled at him so sweetly that his heart gave a leap.

The king was pleased to see that his youngest daughter could not take her eyes off her rescuer, especially when he discovered that the young man was the son of his dearest friend.

Before long there was a great wedding held at the court of the King of Greece, and the merrymaking went on for seven days and seven nights. The mead flowed like water, and each food which was brought to the table was tastier than the last, though all of them were delicious.

After the wedding, Liam Donn returned with his beloved bride to Ireland. The Greek king had rejoiced greatly when Liam Donn saved his youngest daughter, but the Irish king rejoiced even more when he heard the news of his son's brave deed. He greeted Liam Donn in front of the castle gate, which was opened wide to welcome him.

The whole of Ireland feasted for seven days and seven nights, old and young alike, and the royal tables bent beneath the weight of choice foods and drinks. Even the dogs throughout Ireland had a feast, and for seven days and nights they had juicy bones to gnaw.

How the Proud Town of Is
Was Engulfed by the Sea

Long ago the old kingdom of Cornouaille in Brittany was ruled by a powerful king named Grallon. Not only his subjects, but all who knew him, declared that there was no better king in the whole world. Every weary traveller, whether gentleman or pauper, was welcomed at his table. The king himself liked best to sit among minstrels and

poets, who knew much about the wide world, who sang of days past and days to come, of love and of grief, of famous men and places of renown.

Fortune smiled on the king in all things, but still he was often overcome with sorrow when he was alone in the chambers of the castle. The queen had died young, leaving him two daughters, both of them as pretty as a picture. The elder daughter was charming and kind to everyone, and it was no wonder that as soon as she grew into a young woman, the king of the neighbouring kingdom asked for her hand. The princess thought the young king the handsomest young fellow who had ever visited their castle, and from that moment on she would not hear of other suitors. In the end the king was glad to arrange a great wedding for his daughter, at which old and young from nine kingdoms made merry, and King Grallon danced like a young man.

The second princess, whose name was Dahut, had a nature so different that you would never have taken her for the young queen's sister at all. She grew up to be as proud as a peacock. With each day that passed, she became more and more of a worry to her father and all his counsellors and friends, for she treated them with disdain and spite, and showered them with insults. Strangely enough, as she grew more proud, so also she became more and more beautiful, so that she had ten suitors for every finger on her dainty hands. None of them was good enough for her, and she would pick and choose among young and old, and play one admirer off against another. The one thing which would make her eyes light up with satisfaction was to see people arguing over her. Princes, lords and gentlemen were glad to see the last of the castle where Princess Dahut lived with the ladies of her court. When they left, the princess would laugh her head off, and day by day she learnt new tricks with which to tease them all even more.

"The foolishness of youth!" King Grallon sighed more than once, on hearing of the latest malicious trick his daughter had devised. "In time she will surely come to her senses, and not take everything so lightly," he would comfort himself.

One day the king set out hunting with a small group of companions, in order to forget the anxiety his daughter was causing him. As the hunters pushed their way through the dense forest, they suddenly realized they were lost. After wandering about for a long time they came upon a narrow path, which led them to a solitary cottage at the foot of a steep slope. On the threshold a little old man greeted the king like an old friend.

"Tell us who you are, and whether you can show us the way back to the royal city," said the king's first counsellor. "We have long been wandering through thickets so dense that we could not even see the sky above our heads."

"My name is one the world has surely forgotten — I am called Corentin, and I will gladly take you to the road to town. But first of all you must rest a while and take some food, for I see you are tired from your wanderings."

The king was pleased at the man's words, for he had once heard much about the wise hermit Corentin, but the others in his company frowned when they saw the humble cottage, where there was neither food nor a place to rest.

It was as if the old man guessed why the noblemen's faces were clouded. But he told them that the royal cook should make ready his pots and cook some supper, since the gentlefolk had not had a bite to eat since morning. He led the cook to a spring and told him to put water in the great golden cauldron. Then he took a fish from the waters of the spring, tore off a piece of its flesh, and dropped it in the cauldron, returning the wounded creature to the spring. In an instant the fish was made whole again, and swam away happily. The royal cook's face grew darker and darker.

"Are we the king's company, or a band of beggars, that we are to feed on such crumbs? Am I to make myself a laughing stock by cooking such a dish?" he grumbled.

The hermit only smiled.

"Just do as I tell you, and have no fear; you will not regret it. There will be plenty for all. And fill the jugs, too, so that you may be refreshed."

The cook had no choice but to obey, and — lo and behold! In a while the clearing was filled with the smell of a fish soup tastier than he had ever prepared in his life, and from the jugs each of them drank a wine as delicious as honey.

The king ate his fill, refreshed himself with the wine and a little sleep, and then begged the old man, "Leave your hermitage, and return with me to the royal city of Quimper. You shall live in my castle, and take over my affairs of state. Perhaps even my daughter may learn wisdom and humility from you, for you once taught many people how to live honourably and in harmony."

At first Corentin would not hear of returning to the royal city, which he had left long ago, but in the end he allowed himself to be persuaded. The very same day the king handed his castle over to the hermit and went with all his riches to the town of Is, on the sea coast. The beauty of this port was without equal — not even the famous city of Paris was its match. The town was protected from the flood tides by high walls. Their gates were opened and closed only by Princess Dahut herself, who visited the town from time to time; she wore the silver key around her neck, and never took it off. She had once obtained the key from the king of the sea-dragons, by means of powerful spells and magic.

"From this day on the key is yours, and I shall serve you, along with all my subjects," the king of the sea had told her. "But woe betide the town if the key should ever fall into other hands. Remember that from that moment on the sea shall conquer you forever!"

After that the princess would boldly command even the sea-dragons, and on her orders the little people, the korrigans, would come out from under the ground every night. They did her and the town a great many services. They wrought huge gates for the town of Is, and ornamental screens and bridges; then they gilded them, so that it was a wonder the townsfolk were not blinded when the sun shone. They even faced the princess's stables with white, red and black marble, according to the colour of the horses which were stabled there. The korrigans also looked after the horses, feeding and grooming them so well that there was not even a king who had horses so fine.

At dawn the korrigans would feed the sea-dragons, so that they might safely swim from the harbour to the open sea and to distant

shores, bring all the riches they found in shipwrecks there, and take in tow any enemy ships they had captured on the way. In this way the town of Is quickly grew rich beyond compare. The citizens were proud, eating only from silver plates and drinking only from golden goblets, dressing in silk and wool as soft as paper. They danced and made merry on every occasion, but paupers were driven from the city gates with sticks. If the king himself had come to that town dressed in a linen shirt instead of a tunic embroidered with gold, they would have turned him away.

King Grallon was sorely grieved when he saw that neither he nor Corentin could impose his will on the proud city, and in the end the king withdrew to his private chambers, and did not even cross the threshold any more. The people of Is did not know whether their king was alive or dead.

One day an unknown nobleman from a distant land arrived in the town. He rode high on a black stallion, dressed from head to foot in red silk embroidered with gold. From the moment Princess Dahut saw her guest, she was unable to take her eyes off him. The nobleman entered the royal hall, bowed low to the princess, and said, "I greet you, Your Highness, and crave your indulgence. Allow me to stay here in the most beautiful city I have ever seen."

Then he spread out before the princess silken hangings of untold beauty, which he had brought as a gift, and the royal hall was ablaze with the brightness of their splendour. Not only that, but he presented the princess with long strings of pearls the size of plums and precious stones like red apples. Not even she had ever seen such treasures. She smiled sweetly at her guest, entertained him, and danced only with him until midnight. But as midnight approached, the musicians began to play a strange tune, and they played it faster and faster, until the princess and all her guests and servants began to spin round more and more quickly, like so many tops, and were unable to stop for breath.

Then the nobleman in red silk put out his hand and took the silver key from around Dahut's neck.

"You are mine, princess!" he said. "Now you are mine, and from now on you shall be princess of Hell! The town of Is shall also be mine; none shall ever see it again, for it shall be covered forever by the waves of the sea."

In a forgotten corner of the palace, King Grallon was woken from his sleep. It seemed to him that he saw old Corentin standing in the doorway.

"Make haste, my liege, make haste. In the courtyard a saddled horse awaits you. Take it, and ride from the town. Ask no questions now, and do not turn around, or it will go ill with you!"

Confused, the king silently did as Corentin had told him, though it all seemed to be a dream. The demon had already opened the gates in the sea-walls, and the waves of a stormy sea were pouring into the town from all sides. The king's horse was startled; it neighed, thrust its feet against the stones of the courtyard, and with one leap jumped onto the tall cliff above the town. To this day the marks of its hooves can be seen in the rock. Thus it was that good King Grallon was saved, though not a trace of the town of Is or its inhabitants remained above the waves. But they say that when the sea calms down after a storm you can even today find pieces of the untold beauty of its treasures scattered along the shore. And from time to time its mighty walls can be seen beneath the water, a reminder of the forgotten glory of the town of Is, and of the pride of its citizens.

How the Fisherman's Wife Saved the Elf-Queen's Child

One winter's day a young fisherwoman was sitting beside the cradle of her baby son. Outside the wind howled, the sea roared, and the waves crashed against the cliffs. The fisherwoman wept tears of grief.

"My son, my sunshine," she whispered to him softly, "how are we to manage on our own, now that the sea has taken away our bread-winner?"

Suddenly, the hapless woman grew still, for a soft knocking could be heard at the door.

"Who can be knocking so shyly? What stranger is at the door?" she said, fearfully. She opened the door a crack, and in the firelight she saw a little woman as pale as moonlight, holding a baby in her arms. The stranger was scarcely able to walk as she entered the cottage.

"Help me, good woman," she begged. "I am sick and frail; with-out help my child will surely die."

The fisherwoman did not hesitate. She took the small, weak baby girl, all wrapped in a green silk scarf, into her arms and nursed her as if she were her own. Then she placed the baby in the cradle beside her own son, poked up the fire in the grate, and put some of the little flour she still had left in the cottage into her cooking-pot. She added a piece of fish and a few vegetables, and before long a bowl of tasty fish soup was steaming appetizingly on the table. Finally, she made up a bed for the woman, and soon all was quiet in the little cottage, with both women and children fast asleep.

The next morning the young fisherwoman was awakened by the crying of the children. She looked towards the bed, and saw with a start that the woman had gone — disappeared without trace, as if she had never been there. But for the baby girl, crying in the cradle, the fisherwoman would have supposed it had all been a dream. She sighed, took both the children in her arms, and nursed them like a pair of twins. When the little ones had stopped crying, she looked around the cottage, wondering what she was to do now. As she turned towards the table, her eyes came to rest on a bowl full of sieved white flour, a large loaf of bread, a pat of fresh butter and a jar of honey which was tastier than anything the fisherwoman had ever eaten in her life. From the beam over the fireplace hung a smoked salmon, filling the cottage with such a delicious smell that the young woman's mouth began to water. Then she turned her surprised gaze to the bench, and what should she see there but new clothes, both for herself and for the children and silken and woollen bedclothes, feather light. "Only the queen of the elves herself has the power to send such gifts," thought the fisherwoman to herself.

From that day on poverty left the widow's cottage. Now that she was so well cared for, the little girl grew and grew. Her little white face took on a rosy hue, and her green eyes shone like emeralds.

One day, as summer was drawing near, the fisherwoman was singing the children a lullaby, when she heard again the same faint knocking at the door. She got up and opened the door a crack — and there again stood the little woman dressed in green silk. She smiled at the fisherwoman, and in her green eyes there was a glint like starlight on a clear night.

"I come to thank you for saving my daughter's life and mine. Now I am able to look after her myself, so I shall take her back again. But I beg you to come with us this time. Do not be afraid," she added, "tomorrow you shall return home."

Again, the fisherwoman did not hesitate, but put on her headscarf, wrapped her son up warmly, and set out for the mountains with the other woman, each carrying her baby in her arms. They crossed a dark forest and stopped at the foot of the hills. In the thicket in front of them a path suddenly opened up, and soon an iron-bound door opened to let them pass. The thicket closed up behind them, and the blades of grass straightened out where they had trod, as if not even the woodland animals had ever passed that way.

The queen of the elves led the fisherwoman into a blossoming and fertile landscape. The trees there were hung with such sweet fruit that they dripped with scented honey; there were fields of ripening corn, taller than the tallest of fishermen, with ears as long as a horse's head.

In the royal palace there was music playing, sometimes lively and gay, sometimes quiet and stately, and the elves were dancing all their ancient dances. The fisherwoman did not know where to look first: at the carpets and curtains, as soft as the sea foam, or at the rare ornaments of all kinds. Then the elf-queen led her to the head of the table and offered her food and drink, such as not only the fisherwoman had never tasted, but had never adorned the table of even the King of Scotland himself. In the meantime the children slept in a gold cradle, set with precious stones and lined with silk. They must both have been dreaming pleasant dreams, for they smiled happily.

The next day at dawn, the elf-queen thanked the fisherwoman once more.

"Now the time has come for us to part," she told her. "But I shall never forget your kindness. I wish you to have something to remember me by; perhaps the greatest service I can do you is to see to it that you never again see the bottom of the bowl which is on your table, and never again know what it is to be hungry, you or your son. And I have one other gift for you. I have prepared for you a jar containing rare medicaments, such as no man has ever seen. They can cure severe illnesses, heal wounds, mend broken bones. But neither you nor your son shall ever need these remedies. Now go, and live in happiness and contentment."

With that, the royal palace disappeared before the fisherwoman's eyes, and the thicket closed behind her. She was left standing with her son on the black mountain, whence she hurried home as fast as she could.

The fame of the fisherwoman's potions, ointments and healing herbs spread like wildfire across the land. From morning till night, sometimes even from night till morning, she healed the sick and the wounded. More than once she seemed to drive away death itself, and she always had cures enough for both rich and poor, feeding the latter from her own table. But no matter how many medicines or how much food she used up, her table and her shelves remained full. So the fisherwoman and her son, and his children and grandchildren, all lived in good health to a ripe old age. And nowhere along the whole of that long coast was there ever known a doctor as famous as the fisherwoman's son, nor perhaps ever will be.

Master Goban

A long, long time ago there lived in Ireland the celebrated master-builder Goban Saor. There was no one in the whole of Ireland who could carve wood, forge glowing iron, or hew stone like Goban, and there was not a builder to match him. No one built castles more beautiful or more spacious than his. So well did he build, that his towers and halls surely stand to this day, if some fierce enemy has not laid them in ruins.

Goban had two daughters and a son. He paid great attention to his son's upbringing, teaching him everything he knew himself. Though after many years he found out that he was not the boy's true father, he loved him none the less for that.

This was how it all came about:

Goban's nearest neighbour was rich and powerful, but a very strange fellow, called Frannach. He left Goban in peace, and never crossed the river which divided their two houses. Towards his other neighbours, however, near and far, Frannach was less considerate: he quarrelled with them frequently, and he and his nine sons inflicted great damage on them more than once.

The worst time of all was when Frannach's wife was expecting their tenth child. Frannach was pleased to have nine sons, but now he was anxious that his tenth child should be a girl. He swore by the sun and the moon that if his wife did not give birth to a daughter, he would slay both mother and baby. That was just the sort of pagan fellow he was.

Goban Saor's wife was with child at the same time. They already had two daughters, and Goban yearned for a son to whom he might teach his trade.

But one night Goban's wife gave birth to a daughter; an hour before her Frannach's wife had had a son. The wise old midwife told Frannach he had a daughter, and as the old barbarian was leaping with joy, toasting his good fortune, and gleefully spreading the good news, the kind-hearted old woman wrapped his son in a shawl and took him to Goban's wife so that Frannach might do him no harm.

"If only I might have a son, then I should be the happiest woman in the world," sighed Goban's wife.

A little later she gave birth to a healthy daughter.

"Listen," whispered the midwife to Goban's wife. "Let us secretly exchange the babies. The daughter Frannach so desired will be well treated, and Goban will jump for joy when we show him a fine son. But our secret must never get outside these four walls; no one else in the world must know of what has happened. Everything will be all right — you'll see."

The midwife implored the poor mother so long that in the end she let the old woman wrap her daughter in the shawl and take her to Frannach's house. The lad remained under Goban's roof forever.

Both children grew up strong and healthy, and when old Frannach was at home with his daughter he was quite meek and mild, [144] though the moment he set foot outside the door he was no better than he had been in his youth. The girl soon became well known around those parts for her kind heart and her exceptional wisdom. Not even the worldly-wise old folk knew as much as Kathleen Frannach. She caught the eye of many a young man, and a good few of them would have liked nothing better than to make Kathleen their wife. But when they met old Frannach they soon changed their minds.

In the meantime Goban's son learned his father's trade, and was a great help to him. They built many a castle and many a tall tower together. They were both happy and contented, but Goban's wife suddenly took sick. She grew feebler day by day, and lay quite unable to stir from her bed for weeks on end. There was no one to do the work about the house. The two daughters had already married, and suddenly Goban's house lacked a woman's caring hand.

"It's time for you to wed," Goban said to his son one evening. "But be sure you find yourself a wife who is wise, skilful, good and thrifty. Better such a wife without a farthing to her name than a foolish one who might bring a pile of sovereigns into the house."

"Very well, father, I shall do as you ask. I have never regretted taking your good advice," the young man agreed.

Goban nodded silently, and said no more on the matter. But the next week, when it was time for the fair in town, he called his son, gave him a large sheepskin, and told him to sit down in a good place at the fair, where he saw the most people gathered. Then he was to take no notice of what went on around him, only to keep shouting: "Both the price and the sheepskin!" If he found a woman at the fair who paid the price he was asking for the sheepskin, and then returned it to him, but still came out of it well, he was to take her by the hand and lead her straight home. They would soon know if young Goban had really brought home a good wife.

The lad was surprised, but he asked his father only how much he should ask for the sheepskin.

"Just three pence," the master replied.

Early the next morning young Goban set off for town to the fair.

He did just as his father had told him, sat down with the sheepskin in the most crowded place, and began to call out: "Both the price and the sheepskin!"

Everyone at the fair laughed at him, thinking that young Goban was asking a little more than befitted an honest artisan.

Towards evening he returned home, and his father asked him at once, "Well, my son?"

"Nothing, father. I return as I left, only a little hoarse from shouting. Folk laughed at me."

"If you are lucky, they will swallow their mirth. Tomorrow you shall go to the fair again."

The next day young Goban did no better; indeed, almost worse, for by now people thought he was off his head. When he returned the third day with his big sheepskin and kept calling: "Both the price and the sheepskin!" they were ready to put him in chains, thinking that such a madman might do someone harm for laughing at him.

Just as the wise townsfolk were discussing what to do about young Goban, Kathleen Frannach came to the fair. She was not long an orphan; she lived with her brothers, and was sorely tried by them. Apart from the youngest, they were all married now, and her sisters-in-law were envious of the wise Kathleen. When she heard young Goban's shouting, she came up to him, listened for a while, and then smiled at him.

"How much are you asking for the sheepskin?" she asked.

"Just three pence; but I want the skin back again."

The people standing round roared with laughter, but Kathleen had made up her mind.

"If you give me the sheepskin for three pence, I shall return it to you in a little while," she promised. "Just wait a moment."

"Very well," young Goban agreed, and waited patiently.

Kathleen went into the nearest house and borrowed a large pot of boiling water and a pair of shears. The sheepskin grew soft in the steam from the pot, and in a few moments the girl had clipped off all the wool into her apron. For three pence she had a good pile of wool.

Goban leapt to his feet.

[146]

"Come with me," he said, and caught her by the hand.

"Where to?" Kathleen asked.

"To our house. I see that you are the right one; you are the one my father wanted to see, when he said he would like to speak to a wise girl."

Kathleen shook her head, but she liked the handsome Goban, so she went with him.

Old Goban greeted them both warmly when he heard how his son had got on at the fair. As they talked, Goban realized that he had never spoken to such a wise young woman before. In a while he took her to a table with a pile of money on it.

"What do you say to that?" he asked her.

"What should I say? A pile like that is a good thing, especially if it grows larger. Better for it to be on the table than for there to be nothing on it."

Master Goban was most pleased with her answer.

In a while he took Kathleen out into the garden and showed her the wall around the house, and some new outbuildings.

"What have you to say about our work? Do you think we should have done it better?"

"Even if you were to knock it all down, you could scarcely build it better a second time. But why do you ask?" Kathleen said suddenly, "for you know that a good craftsman's work speaks for itself."

Master Goban smiled with satisfaction; he could see that he would find no better wife for his son in the whole world. So he proposed to her on his son's behalf.

The young pair were as happy as could be. But Goban's wife was even happier when she found out whom young Goban had brought into the house.

Famous Master Goban had lived well since his youth, for he was born under a lucky star, and had skilled hands, a wise head and a kind heart. And with such a father, young Goban, too, had always done well for himself; but neither of them had ever been so content as when Kathleen came into the house. Even old Goban had a lot to learn from her.

The two Gobans had so much work that they could scarcely

manage to do it all. Their services were in great demand, for there were no other builders more renowned. But still Kathleen was able to give them good advice when they were building a tower. She had brought them their midday meal, and she stood looking for a while as they carefully lined up every stone as they laid it on the wall.

"Husband," said Kathleen quietly, "do not be angry with me; perhaps what I say is foolish. But it seems to me that it would be simpler to measure two corners only, then to stretch a piece of string between them. Would you not find it quicker?"

"Oh, my child, my child!" cried old Goban. Kathleen thought he was angry at her for interfering, but in fact he could not admire her cleverness enough. The Gobans took her advice, and did as much work in a single day as they would normally take a week to complete.

The Gobans had always been famous, but now the fame of their work spread seven times as far as before, for they did the work of a dozen skilled masons. Their renown even reached over the sea and across England. A certain powerful lord lived there at the time. One day he resolved to build the finest castle in the world, and he was determined to employ no other builders than the Gobans. He could think of nothing else but how to get them to come to England. Straight away he sent for them, promising a huge reward when their work was completed. He was not concerned as to where he would get so much money, since he was forging a cunning scheme.

When the Gobans received word that the mighty lord wished them to build the finest castle in all England, and heard that he was offering more wages than they had ever earned in their lives, they quickly took up his offer. Kathleen made ready all they needed for their journey, and then whispered some words of advice to her husband.

"Husband, pay attention to the servants of the house. Sing with them, dance with them, joke with them; invite them to take ale with you, and then listen carefully to what they say. I have heard tell that many good builders cross the sea, but that few of them ever return. They disappear as if the ground had swallowed them up."

"Very well, Kathleen; since I wish to return to you, I shall keep my eyes and ears open."

The next morning early, the master and his son set out on their long journey. They strode along briskly, and walked for a long time, but somehow the road passed slowly.

"Shorten our journey!" the father told his son.

So young Goban lengthened his stride, but his father stopped him.

"If you know no other way, then let us return home."

Young Goban shook his head, but he turned obediently. By evening they were back home again. Kathleen was surprised to see them, but she said nothing, only heated some water for them to wash off the dust of the road, and prepared them a good supper. That night, when her husband told her why they had returned, she laughed.

"Why did you not tell your father an interesting story? The journey would have passed more quickly."

The next day they set off even earlier, and when young Goban began to tell some good tales, the old master, too, remembered all manner of stories to tell his son, and the journey passed so swiftly that before they knew it they were at the sea. They took a boat to England, and set about their work. By the time a third of the building work was done, all those who saw them declared that they had never seen such a master of masters as old Goban, nor such a merry and obliging youth as his son. By the time the new castle was almost complete, young Goban knew about almost everything that went on in the old castle.

Late one evening a frightened maid from the house came hurrying up to young Goban.

"Goban, I shall never sleep soundly again if I do not warn you of the danger you are in. But be sure not to reveal that I told you of it, for the gentlemen would surely kill me too. I heard the master tell the mistress that the day you finish the new castle he will hurl you both into the deepest dungeon, so that you may never again see the light of day, or ever build another castle which might compare with his."

Young Goban thanked the girl, and promised her that he and his father would never tell a soul of what she had whispered to him as long as they lived.

"It is well that we know what reward we may expect for our labours, my son," said old Goban, when he heard of it. "But I think we can get the better of the scoundrel if we set our minds to it."

The Gobans knew that so long as the castle was not completed they were in no danger, so they built on contentedly, quickly and well.

When at last the work was finished, the lord surveyed his new castle from its deepest dungeon to its tall roof, and he was well pleased.

"The castle is beautiful, beautiful," he said with satisfaction.

"Indeed it is," the master agreed.

"Tell me true, master," said the lord, turning to old Goban, "have you ever seen or heard of a finer castle?"

"In truth, my lord, your castle is the finest in the world. I have neither seen nor heard of a finer one. But . . ."

"But what? Speak!" thundered the lord.

"I was about to tell you when you interrupted. In Leinster there is a royal castle with a taller and more beautiful tower."

"And could you not build me a tower finer than the one at Leinster?"

"Indeed I could," replied the master, "why not? We have built your castle: give us the reward we were promised, and we shall go home for the necessary implements, then return and build your tower."

"No, no. It would take you too long, and too many days would be lost. Stay here; eat, drink and rest, and I shall send my own son with some servants to bring what you require."

"Dear me, I don't know, I don't know," said the old man.

"Just say what you need!" the lord urged him.

"Very well," agreed Goban at last. "Let your son go to my house, where he will find a young housewife. She shall see to everything, for my wife is sick."

Soon the lord's son was standing before the master, ready for his journey.

"Tell me what I am to bring, master Goban."

"Ask the young woman for a trickfurratrick and for guilagincunning."

"What a strange language that Irish of yours is!" the young man replied, taken aback. "Would you mind repeating that?"

"A trickfurratrick and guilagincunning. Will you remember?"

"I shall," the young man promised, and set out at once for Ireland. He sailed across the sea, found Goban's house, and was soon standing in front of Kathleen herself.

"Greetings from master Goban and his son. They have finished the castle, but have yet to build a tower. My father wishes it to be taller and more beautiful than that on the royal castle at Leinster, and I am to take the things they need. Goban asks you for a trickfurratrick and guilagincunning."

Kathleen listened carefully to the young man's words, and knew at once that young and old Goban were in some great danger in England, since they asked for a trick for a trick and for guile against cunning. She smiled sweetly at the young gentleman, sat him down at table, set food and drink before him, and saw to the servants' well-being also. After some time she said:

"Goban's tools are in the great chest over in the corner. Stand up on the stool and have a look inside."

Kathleen opened the big chest, and the young gentleman leaned right over into it. Then Kathleen jumped up, pushed him inside, and banged the lid shut. After that she locked the door, opened the window, and called out to the servants:

"Return to your master and tell him the young gentleman will remain here. No harm shall come to him if master Goban and his son return safely with the wages they were promised. Then he shall go free. But if your lord does not fulfil my conditions, he will never see his son again."

When the servants returned to England with this message, the lord saw that there was nothing for it but to reward the Gobans generously and send them home. He grated his teeth as he counted out the sovereigns, but his son's life was dearer to him than all treasures.

So, with Kathleen's help, the Gobans returned safely to Ireland. They all loved Kathleen more dearly than ever after that, though master Goban wondered more than once how wild old Frannach had come to have such a wise daughter, so wise that there was no other woman in the world to compare with her. And when, one day, he said this out loud in front of his sick wife, her poor tongue was untied, and she told him the whole truth from beginning to end.

Master Goban leapt up and embraced his wife.

"Do you know how happy I am that the wisest woman in all the world is our own daughter? And see how Frannach's youngest son has learnt an honest trade in our house, instead of brigandry like his elder brothers. Isn't that work as good at least as building the most beautiful tower in the world?"

And the Gobans lived happily for the rest of their lives.

How the Beautiful Helen Became Queen of Rome

Once upon a time, a long, long time ago, a handsome young king was ruler of Rome. He was not only wise and merry, but had looked danger in the face more than once, and still was kind-hearted through and through. No wonder everyone simply called him

Maxim, though he was a mighty monarch and ruled over a great many kingdoms.

One day the young king set off with some companions and servants to go hunting. At noon, when the sun was high in the sky, the king's company retired to a clearing to rest, for they were exhausted from the heat. The king's eyelids grew heavy, and weariness poured over him. His head sank onto his hunting tunic, and in a moment he fell fast asleep. A strange dream came to him. He saw himself sitting on a horse and riding alongside a river until he came to its source in the high mountains. From there he climbed on to dizzy heights, and finally crossed a steep-sided ridge between snow-covered peaks. He was greatly anxious as he travelled, more than once losing hope of ever returning alive from among the icy rocks. When at last he safely reached the valley below, he found himself in a broad landscape of fertile fields, pretty villages, rich towns and proud castles with many towers. At the mouth of a great river a harbour full of ships appeared. The largest of the ships had a golden deck with silver rails, and its poop was of rare wood, with rails of ornately carved bone.

The king could see neither flag nor crew, from which he might discern whose ship was anchored there, nor where it was sailing for. He leapt from his horse, and curiosity drove him onto the vessel's bridge. As he stepped on board, the sails filled and the ship got under way and made for the open sea. The king, in his dream, was not even surprised at this.

By and by the ship came to the shore of a country more delightful than the king had ever seen in his life. On the horizon, mountains soared skywards, enclosing the land like a garden. These mountains stretched as far as the eye could see, and on the plain at their foot a huge river crossed fields as green as emeralds. On the crest of a knoll stood a golden castle, as lovely as a dream. The gates opened to let King Maxim pass, and he crossed a courtyard and entered a large hall. Its walls were hung with splendid carpets, and on the floor of precious stones there were golden stools beside silver tables. On them sat two players engrossed in a game of chess, the pieces on the table between them richly inlaid with gold and silver. No one noticed the arrival of a guest. Then a golden-haired woman in white robes entered the hall: she was more charming and more beautiful than the pearl of Roman womanhood. It was she who first caught sight of the newcomer.

"Welcome, my dearest," she said in a voice like a golden bell, and, smiling, she ran up to him and threw herself into his arms as though she had been waiting for him for a long time.

At that instant there was a neighing of horses and a barking of dogs, and the king was jerked out of his dreaming. He could scarcely believe he was lying in a forest glade, with only his hunting party around him. A moment before he had been happier than he had ever been in his life, and he was close to despair that his dream should have dissolved like so much mist. Then he swung himself into the saddle and trotted slowly back towards the city.

From the time King Maxim awoke in that forest glade, he was quite changed, as though someone had cast a spell on him. Soon even those closest to him scarcely recognized him. He had once been the merriest of the merry company, and now he would scarcely show his face among his guests. When there was merrymaking and all were feasting, dancing and singing, the king would simply frown and retire in silence to his chamber. He hoped that the beautiful woman might again appear to him in a dream, that woman he so yearned for that she filled his thoughts both night and day. But he had no idea where the country he had sailed to in his dream might be, or how he might get there. He only believed that such a vivid dream could not have come to him just like that, and he waited and waited for some sign of where in the wide world he should travel to.

In time the oldest of the king's counsellors, who had long since been a friend of Maxim's father, spoke to the young man.

"My liege, we are all most concerned that you are sad and listless, that you see neither good nor ill around you, and that you walk amongst us as if you were a ghost. Only tell me what illness afflicts you, and we shall surely find a cure for it."

"I am not sick, and if I were, then there could be no cure for me."

"How do you know that, my liege? Rome is full of wise physicians. They will surely know what to do even with your disease. Only tell us what it is that torments you."

"Very well! Call all my counsellors from the whole of the land; I shall consult them to see if they can find me a medicament to make me merry again."

When all the counsellors from near and far had assembled in the royal hall, the king addressed them:

"Gentlemen, you have always been good friends and counsellors to me; now hear what I have to tell you. I do not suppose any of you will be able to advise me. While I was out hunting, I had a dream more vivid than any in my life." Then he related how he had found the beautiful woman in the golden castle, adding at the last: "If I am not able to find that golden-haired beauty who greeted me as the most intimate of friends, I shall not pass a single day or night in peace, nor shall I be a ruler any more, nor a companion to my friends."

The counsellors put their heads together, then shook them this way and that, until at last the oldest of them again came before the king:

"My liege, you wished to hear our counsel; we are agreed that the best course would be to send envoys to all parts of the world, that in a year and a day they might find that golden castle in a strange land which appeared to you in your dream. You will not know whether or not your envoys will return with good news, but the very hope of it must raise your spirits a little at least."

The king could think of nothing better to do himself, so he took the advice of his counsellors and soon envoys were setting off in all directions. But all hope was in vain: in a year's time all of them returned exhausted and with heads hung low. They had searched many lands from end to end, but had found no sign of the castle they were looking for, nor of the golden-haired woman. The king began to waste away with grief; he did not even want to live, if he could not find out something at least about the beautiful woman of his dream.

By and by the oldest of the counsellors came to the king again, and again coaxed him, "My liege, why do you despair because our first expedition did not succeed? The world is wide and stretches far, and our envoys require something to put them on the right track.

You should return to the place where you had the dream. There you will surely remember something which might give the envoys some clue as to where they are to search."

"Very well," the king agreed. Again he drew strength from renewed hope, and so he set out with his whole company to go hunting. They found the clearing in the forest where the king had slept, and before long they came across a river close by.

"Perhaps fortune will not leave me this time," sighed the king. "It was from this place that I set off in my dream, going upstream along the river until I reached its source in the high mountains. Directly above it was a tall, steep ridge which joined two snow-covered peaks. It was only there that it was possible to cross between the icy rocks."

So it was that, little by little, the king remembered how he had wandered in his dream until he came to the foot of the knoll where the golden castle stood.

Before long a new party of envoys, with the oldest of the counsellors at its head, set out upstream along the river. They crossed the mountains into the kingdom of France without misfortune, and by the seashore found a ship just like the one King Maxim had described. The moment the last of the party had gone on board, the ship sailed for the open sea. It skudded across the waves with the speed of an arrow, steering its own course to a port near to which there was a golden castle standing on a tall knoll. Now the Romans were able to see for themselves that the king had not been deceived in his dream, and that no ordinary adventure was awaiting them. They entered the castle, and stood in the doorway of a large hall. Once again there were golden stools and silver tables standing on the jewel-studded floor. On the stools sat players engrossed in chess, and not far from them an old king sat on a golden stool, hammering a pattern into soft, red gold. At his feet sat a golden-haired woman, as fresh as the morning and as pretty as a picture. Now not even the oldest counsellor was surprised that King Maxim had lost his head for her, and that he saw her image before him day and night.

The envoys bowed low.

"Greetings, noble lords; greetings to you also, future queen of

Rome," the old counsellor addressed those who were sitting there.

"Gentlemen," the golden-haired woman replied, "I see that you are envoys from a far-off land, and we should like to welcome you as befits your state. But first tell me why you mock me, who am not known to you."

"Forgive us, Your Highness; we should never dare to make fun of you. We have come half way across the world, sent here by our master, the King of Rome. He saw you in a dream, most noble lady, and has been unable to rest since then; he does not even wish to live if he cannot see you with his own eyes. Now tell us, my lady, if you will return with us to Rome to become Queen of Rome, or if our king is to travel to this far country to visit you."

"Gentlemen, now I believe that you are not making fun of me. But you know yourselves that dreams are like gentle breezes that pass in the twinkling of an eye. Perhaps when your king sees me he will wonder how I could have enchanted him so in his dream. But if he indeed loves me as much as you say, he will surely gladly come here."

The envoys rested in the golden castle and refreshed themselves from their long journey. They learned that they were the guest of Eudav, King of Wales, respected for his wisdom and valour by the rulers of lands near and far. The golden-haired girl was his daughter Helen, and the two chess-players were his sons Kynan and Edeon, who had just returned from their schooling.

The next day the royal missives took their leave of their hosts and hurried homewards. They rested neither by day nor by night until they sighted their capital city stretching from horizon to horizon.

King Maxim was already awaiting them impatiently.

"I thank you for your services," he addressed them when they entered the royal hall. "Tell me quickly whether or not you found the golden-haired one in that distant country, and what message you bring me from her and her father. Do not hesitate to add what reward you ask for your great endeavour. But if you have not found her, then let me sleep, for maybe I shall at least dream of her again."

"We have found her, my liege," the oldest of the counsellors replied. "We shall take you to her at once, across mountains and val- [158]

leys and the wide sea, for it is the will of Princess Helen of Wales. She is worthy to live by your side, and none of us will ever see a woman more fit to become Queen of Rome."

No wonder that after hearing these words King Maxim was soon setting out on the long journey. He had the finest jewels and ornaments selected from the royal treasury, and the rarest cloths, books and beverages were made ready, the king himself seeing to it that all was carefully packed into their saddle-bags. Then the long train of riders set out from Rome to France. When they arrived at the harbour, the exquisite ship with its golden deck and silver rails was waiting for them, and before long it had carried them to the shore of the distant island kingdom.

King Maxim did not know whether to laugh or to cry with joy, when he suddenly saw the roofs of the golden castle flashing in the sunlight from the crest of the hill on which it stood.

"This is the countryside I saw in my dream!" he cried, and was unable to contain his impatience until he entered the hall of the castle. Everything in it was just as it had been in his dream: on a floor of precious stones stood golden stools and silver tables, where a pair of players were engaged in a game of chess, and the old king sat bent over his fine metal-work. The golden-haired woman in a white robe raised her head and smiled sweetly at them as they arrived. The king addressed her softly:

"Greetings, Queen of Rome, and greetings to you, too, gentlemen!"

The golden-haired girl rose, went to meet him and embraced him. King Maxim was not sure whether he was dreaming again, or if this time it was real.

The next day King Eudav said to his son-in-law-to-be, "My son, I have something I would ask of you. I am old, and my sons are still boys. I should be happy if you could stay here for a while after your marriage, and travel the length and breadth of my country, from the northern sea to the Irish, so that you may judge where more valiant men are needed, and where wise heads are too few, that there might be peace and order in this country and people might live in contentment and harmony. If you perform this difficult task, then my sons

[160]

will learn from you all that a good king should know. Then I can take my leave of this world with a light heart, and you shall return to Rome. You are not needed so urgently there as you are here."

King Maxim agreed to do as Eudav asked, and for a whole seven years he roamed Wales, sometimes fighting against enemies with his company, sometimes bringing good counsel to settle quarrels; he introduced many new things to Wales, and learnt not a few things himself. More than once he sat in the company of wise counsellors; he would also go hunting and make merry, so that a month by Helen's side passed more quickly than had a single day in Rome.

When Maxim stayed away from Rome so long, a new king was placed upon the throne. And the first thing the new ruler did was to send Maxim a message saying that he was not to return to Rome, or it would be the worse for him! The letter was sent by fast messenger. When Maxim read it, he began to shake with anger. He sat down at the table and wrote an even shorter letter, simply saying that the intruder had nothing to look forward to when he did return.

That very same day King Maxim gathered together his most faithful followers, took Queen Helen by the hand, said farewell to the old king and to his brothers-in-law, and sailed for France. He hurried across mountain and valley, until at last he made camp before the walls of Rome. The people of the city were terribly afraid, and no one dared open a single gate and greet their returning king as was befitting after his long journey. He laid siege to the city for a whole year, for he wished the Romans to welcome him themselves, and was reluctant to set brother against brother. The rumour of this got back to Wales, and from that moment Kynan and Edeon did not rest until they had gathered the pick of their warriors to go to the aid of their sister and brother-in-law. Their numbers were not great, but each of them was so courageous that he was worth a dozen soldiers of the enemy.

Late one afternoon the tents of an army began to spring up close to Maxim's camp, like mushrooms after the rain.

"Who is this that has come?" asked the king, anxiously.

"It seems to me that my brothers have come to our aid," replied the queen, joyfully. The next day at dawn she leapt upon a horse and set off to find out if her eyes had deceived her, or if those really were Welsh standards she had seen in the nearby camp. Words cannot tell of the joy her brothers felt at seeing their sister alive and well.

"Brother-in-law, take us to a place from which we can observe the Roman army and life in the town without being seen ourselves," they begged Maxim, when they had greeted each other happily.

That evening the brothers returned to camp as merry as if they had won a great battle. After dark they measured the height and depth of the fortifications around the city, then sent skilled woodcutters and carpenters into the nearby forest to make a ladder for each soldier. Maxim only shook his head.

"You see, brother-in-law," smiled the princes, "we saw a strange thing, which gave us comfort. At noon, when both you and the other one who calls himself King of Rome refresh yourselves with food and sleep, all activity in the city suddenly comes to a halt. Even the generals rest, and the soldiers sleep. That is when our time will come — and be sure that we shall not miss it."

In the morning the Welshmen ate well, and then only waited. As the sun climbed to the top of the sky at noon, the leaders in the city and in Maxim's camp retired into the shade to rest. All movement ceased, and soon there was quiet everywhere, except in the tents beneath the walls. There the Welshmen quietly made ready their ladders; then they propped them against the walls, and climbed over them like so many cats. The sleepy Roman soldiers had no time to grab their weapons or to raise their shields, and soon the fortifications were in the hands of the attackers. By evening the city had been overrun.

"Dear brother-in-law and King of Rome, we hand over your city to you. Rule again in peace over your mighty empire," the princes announced in Maxim's camp the next morning.

King Maxim and his wife thanked the young princes kindly for their help, and there was joy without bounds in the camp. The people of the liberated city greeted them everywhere with flowers; wine flowed like water, and spits of tasty roasting meat turned in every courtyard.

Finally, as the two princes were taking leave of their sister and brother-in-law, King Maxim asked them, "Tell me truly, my trusty helpers; why did you enter the city alone, leaving me resting in my camp like some frail old man who was unable to take hold of a weapon?"

"Simply because it was work for Welshmen and not for you," replied Prince Kynan. "For you the gates of Rome were to open from the inside, which is just what happened. The people greeted you with song, flowers and wine, not with the clash of weapons."

"You delivered our city, and we are bound to you in gratitude," said King Maxim. "So take with you as a mark of our esteem and brotherly love the whole of my bodyguard. They have served me through thick and thin for many years, and they will serve you likewise." With that the brothers-in-law parted.

Who knows how long the brothers Kynan and Edeon wandered, seeing life in many different countries? They themselves did not count months, only good deeds. They righted many a wrong with the

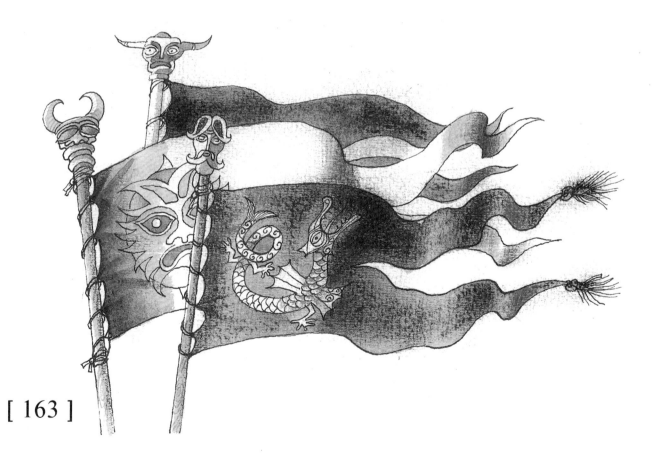

sword; elsewhere they helped by wise words. Then, at last, Edeon was overcome with homesickness.

"Brother, we have wandered long enough, done deeds enough, and seen all we need of the world. Let us return home."

Kynan only shook his head.

"But we are happy, and have everything we could wish for. Our father is still alive, and does not need us at home."

So, for the first time in their lives, the brothers parted from each other for a long time. Edeon took ship with his company and returned to the golden castle on the hill. After his father's death he became King of Wales, earning renown for his kingdom throughout the world. Kynan remained where he was happiest, and from then on that land was called Brittany. King Maxim and Queen Helen lived happily in Rome for the rest of their lives. There was not another queen to equal the golden-haired Helen from Wales, whose beauty and goodness shone like a jewel set in gold. And while King Maxim ruled Rome, peace and concord reigned between his empire and the kingdom of Wales on the distant island, so that when Roman and Welshman met, their swords always remained sheathed.

How the Korrigans Dried
their Gold

Once, a long time ago, the little people, or korrigans, as the Bretons called them, would go into the houses of peasants, or even into great mansions. They climbed in through the chimney at night or squeezed through tiny holes and cracks in the walls, and helped good folk everywhere, who would leave food and milk for them. While they were about it they often played roguish tricks. During the night they would throw handfuls of gold pieces from their underground treasures on the sea shore. When people saw them they would come running, toiling away to collect every last little piece from even the most inaccessible places, from crevices in the rocks not even big enough for a bird to nest in, and digging up great piles of sand and rejoicing like little children at each little grain of gold they put in their baskets and bags. Sometimes they even fought over pieces of the treasure, and returned home battered and bruised, scarcely able to shut all the doors and windows so that no one might see how much gold they had had the good fortune to pick up. Then they would tip out onto the table from their baskets and purses ordinary, wet stones and sand. At that moment there would usually be a sniggering from the chimney as if the little people would die laughing. Then the disappointed victims would only sigh, "Ah me, what a waste of time! The korrigans' gold is no good to anyone."

But the good folk, who left the korrigans a piece of scone even when times were hard, and made an honest living from cows and horses, often received real gold, tinkling with a sound as clear as a bell.

The korrigans and the people lived like that for a long time, until a great famine came upon the whole land. All of a sudden the poor people had nothing to put on their tables or into the mangers in their stables. The rich first of all sold their fine cows and horses, and drove donkeys home from market. A long-eared donkey would eat even docks and thistles, and would carry such a load that he could scarcely be seen beneath it, so that it looked as if a pile of reeds or baggage was walking along the road. In this way the big landowners just about managed to keep their heads above water. But the korrigans — who knows why — could not stand donkeys, and no longer went onto farms where they were kept, or helped to look after the cows, so that there was less and less milk, and everyone lamented that times were hard. As always, the poor were hardest hit, and when they had nothing else left they were forced to sell their only horse or cow for a few pence. Then they were overtaken by hunger, and the next step was a beggar's stick.

"Nothing for it now but to go begging!" sighed farmer Le Calvez, like his neighbours. "Nothing else can save us, if I do not sell the mare at the fair tomorrow."

"Father, somehow we shall manage even with the mare," begged his eldest son. "We shall put her out to graze at night, and in the daytime we two shall do some work in the mill and on the big farms. If we get rid of her, we shall be worse off than ever."

The farmer simply hid his head in his hands in silence, and with a heavy heart the young man led the mare off to its night pasture. He did not sleep a wink till dawn, searching up and down for places with a little greenery to graze the horse. When morning came, he took hold of the mare's bridle, and they slowly wended their way home. At the foot of an old castle the lad suddenly froze as if his feet were stuck in the ground. In the meadow, where the first rays of the sun were falling, he saw the glint of so much gold that it was a wonder he was not blinded by the glare. The korrigans were just bringing sacks full of treasure out from under the ground to dry it in the morning sun.

"What do you want, young fellow?" cried one of the little people.

"Nothing, nothing: I am just taking the mare from her night pasture," answered the startled young man. "But if you were to give me just one gold piece, so that we should not have to sell her, we should never forget it," he added, boldly, when he saw how much treasure there was there. The korrigan surveyed him from head to toe and then from toe to head.

"Very well," he said after a while, "but mind you don't sell the mare and bring a donkey into the stable!" And with his little rake he skilfully scraped up a pile of gold pieces, and scooped them into a small linen bag for the lad.

There is no describing the joy which reigned in the Le Calvez household. The farmer and his son went off to the mill to buy flour, and the farmer's wife fired the oven ready to make some bread.

The miller shook his head when he saw the gold in Le Calvez's hand and the mare in front of the mill.

"Where did you get the money, if you have not sold the horse?" he roared at the farmer. "Have you been out robbing in the night?"

The Le Calvezs had nothing to hide, so the young man told the miller how he had come by the gold. The miller just shook his head, treated his customers with deference, and could not wait for night-fall. At daybreak, when the cock crew for the third time at the mill, the miller was waiting beneath the old castle with a big flour-sack under each arm, hoping the korrigans would appear with their treasure. And suddenly there they were, coming out of the ground like ants, carrying such heavy baskets and sacks that it was a wonder their backs did not break under the load. The miller hardly dared breathe. The little folk stopped suddenly, and the oldest of them, his hair as white as milk, called out angrily to the miller, "What do you want? What are you doing here? Why do you not leave us in peace?"

"I? Nothing," cowered the miller. "That is, I just came to ask for a little gold, since we are all afflicted with such want!"

The korrigan was so angry when he heard these words that sparks flew from his eyes.

"How dare you tell us that you are afflicted by famine? Just you wait, you shall have as much gold as you can carry!"

Before the miller knew what was happening, blows from the korrigans' sticks were raining down on his back. They beat him like a sheaf of rye as long as he was able to stand on his feet.

Meanwhile others had led away the miller's horse and filled his flour-sacks with stones. Now they tied them on his back and sent him home.

Battered and bruised, and bent beneath the weight of the stones, the miller was more dead than alive when he finally arrived back at the mill. He could not get the sacks off his back on the way — it was as if they were growing there. It was a week before he left his bed, and even then he could scarcely manage to drag himself about the mill.

But on the Le Calvez farm they never knew want any more. Every night the korrigans led the mare out to graze, rode about on her, cleaned her and brushed her till her coat shone like gold. Only then did they drink the milk and eat the fresh scones that were always ready for them, licking their lips with delight. No wonder that with such help as that young Le Calvez soon had the finest horses for many miles around, and good fortune and contentment smiled upon him from every corner.

Foxglove and the Little People

In a quiet valley a little way above a village, there once lived a poor basket-maker. The young man was not greatly troubled by poverty, for he had clever hands and had learnt an honest trade. There was none for miles around could weave baskets and cradles, stools and hives from wicker and straw like he could. But what did trouble him greatly was that a large hump had grown on his back from the time

he had fallen down a high flight of steps when he was a boy. The children would point their fingers at him, and call him Foxglove, for in summer he always wore foxglove flowers in his hat, and the red bells would bob up and down above his head in a funny sort of way, as if they were ringing. But there were many folk who were afraid of the humpback, saying that pixies wore foxglove flowers instead of caps, and that it was wise to beware of the basket-maker, for he surely did not wear those flowers in his hat for nothing. And though they spoke ill of the kind-hearted young man, in fact he would not have hurt a fly.

The basket-maker was annoyed by the shouting of the children, who never tired of calling after him, so he would set off for the fair at dawn, and return late in the evening, when the noisy youngsters were all asleep.

One night he was returning thus from the fair, and some distance before the village he left the road and turned onto a path through the fields. He was tired from the hubbub of the town and from his long trek, and he could scarcely put one foot in front of the other as he walked along beside a dried-up stream. There was water in this ditch only when it rained, but now it was dry, with tall, fresh grass growing there, even in high summer. Small wonder the basket-maker felt like sitting down in it to take a rest. He sank into the grass, rested his chin on his knees, and watched sadly as a bright moon rose. Just then he heard quiet music coming from the ditch. At first he thought it was his imagination, but then he heard clearly how a merry song was coming from under the gorse. He listened carefully, and it seemed to him he had never heard anything like it in his life. There were many voices repeating the same words over and over again:

"Monday, Tuesday,

Monday, Tuesday . . ."

But they chanted them in a merry way, sometimes quickly, sometimes slowly; when they had been singing and singing their song for a long time, simply repeating "Monday, Tuesday . . .", they fell silent for a moment. Then they started again.

The young basket-maker hardly dared breathe lest he interrupt the song. After he had been listening for a long time, he began to hum very quietly. In the end he could not resist, and when the singing stopped for a moment, he sang out in a clear voice:

". . . and Wednesday
and Thursday . . ."

When the singers beneath the ground heard the lad's clear voice, they were overjoyed that he should sing with them. They ran out from beneath the bushes, gathered round him, clapped their hands and leaped about, calling to him and pulling him with them under the ground to entertain and cheer them with his song. The basket-maker did not resist, and as swiftly as the wind they led him into an underground palace. It was more beautiful than anything he had ever seen. Thousands of lights shone there, and everything in the palace was of pure gold and silver, gleaming fit to blind the young visitor. Little folk dressed all in silk, with red caps on their heads just like foxglove flowers, sat the shy young lad down at a table, offered him choicest foods and beverages of all kinds, and when he had taken a look around him and become a little surer of himself, began to sing. And the basket-maker joined in with them. Whenever they sang "Monday, Tuesday", he added ". . . and Wednesday, and Thursday". Not even the oldest of the little people could remember such entertainment. In the end the king of the elves thanked the young basket-maker for coming to visit them, and asked if he had a wish they might fulfil.

"There is only one thing I should like," replied the basket-maker. "But it is a great deal to ask."

"Speak out boldly," the elf-king told him.

"I don't want to have a hump any more!"

The king of the elves patted the lad on his hump, and then all the singers and merrymakers in the palace did the same. With each pat he seemed to grow lighter. Surprised, the basket-maker looked around, and saw his hump lying at his feet. He blinked, thinking it was just a dream. His head was spinning with happiness; then he fell into a deep sleep.

Bright sunshine woke Foxglove up. He looked around him, and jumped to his feet when he saw that he had slept in the grass above the stream. But how lightly he could jump without his hump! He whooped with joy, broke into a run, and leapt across the stream like a little boy; he still could not believe that his back was as straight as a plank. When people saw him, they could not believe their eyes. Foxglove the humpback was now a fine-looking young man, more handsome than any other in the village. There were many who did not even recognize him.

Old and young gathered round the basket-maker, and each of them patted him on the back at least once, until he began to be afraid that so much patting might make his hump grow again. But nothing of the sort happened, and afterwards he drank to his neighbours' health.

The fame of the humpback's straight back spread through the countryside. Gentlemen and their servants, rich and poor, all spoke of nothing else, and some even refused to believe it possible.

One day the basket-maker was weaving in front of his cottage, whistling merrily as he worked. An old woman, a stranger, stopped in front of him, and asked if he did not happen to know where the young man who had been a humpback lived.

"Here," replied the basket-maker. "I used to have a hump."

The old woman looked him up and down three times to see if the handsome young fellow was not making fun of her, then she told him why she was looking for him. Her sister's only son was also a humpback, and this troubled them all greatly. If he would tell them how he had got rid of his hump, they would give him all the silver pieces they had saved up.

"I do not need your silver pieces; I will tell anyone who cares to hear." And the kind-hearted basket-maker told the old woman the whole story, from start to finish. The woman thanked him for his good advice, and hurried home, so that she might send her nephew as soon as possible to the place from which the basket-maker had heard the little people singing.

But the other humpback had not only an ugly hump, but also a wicked heart. When he heard he would have to go so far, he whimpered and complained until the two old women had to load him onto a handcart and push him right to the ditch. He was unconcerned that they almost collapsed with exhaustion. He sat stuffing himself with bread and smoked mutton, and when he heard no singing, he muttered and grumbled, and almost scared the elves right away with his trying complaints. When he was quiet at last, he heard a soft singing from under the earth. But this time the little people's singing was a great deal more beautiful than before, when the basket-maker had heard them, for their song was a good deal longer.

They sang from their hearts:

"Monday,

Tuesday

and Wednesday

and Thursday . . ."

In a while they sang the song again, and then again. But then the impatient humpback could contain himself no longer. He shouted at the top of his voice:

"Friday, Saturday, Sunday!"

Perhaps he thought that the louder he joined in the song and the more words he supplied, the more generous the elves would be. Maybe they would not only straighten his back and throw in a new suit of clothes, as they had done with the basket-maker, but give him a purse full of gold and silver to boot.

At that instant the song fell silent, as if the loud words had snapped all the musicians' strings. The little folk ran out from under the ground and gathered round the intruder. But they did not invite him to join them in their revels and cheer them with his song, nor did they offer him choice food and drink.

"What are you doing here, you uncouth fellow! Why are you shouting in the night, and spoiling our revels?" the elves demanded, angrily.

"Stop your prattle!" the spiteful fellow snarled at the little folk. "It is you who are shouting, not I. Whoever would put up with your eternal: Monday, Tuesday and Wednesday and Thursday, over and over again?"

Now the elves got really angry. The twenty strongest went back underground and brought the basket-maker's hump. Then they lifted it over their heads and slapped it on the uncouth fellow's back as he sat there, startled. So now he had two humps instead of one.

In the morning the two old women found the poor fellow more dead than alive. They carted him off home, cursing the elves and Foxglove the basket-maker all the way. But all to no avail: what was done could not be undone.

How Janet Fought
against the Queen of the Elves

Once, a very long time ago, the elves not only lived under the ground, coming out at night to sing, dance or even feast in quiet spots, but they also had their own forests and meadows, where strangers were not allowed to set foot. So that no one might disturb them in their forests and glades, they had knights who kept out intruders. It was these that people were most afraid of, for they punished inquisitive folk severely. All of a sudden people would be led off to the far side of bogs, after which they would only just be able to make their way home after several days, or

dragged into thorny thickets, where they would be pricked all over. No one could tell what mischief the elf-knights would think up next to use against nosy folk who displeased the rulers of the underground kingdom. The elves could often be persuaded to relent with a pleasant word or a song, but their knights were not to be trifled with.

No wonder there were few people bold enough to venture into Carterhaugh Wood, for it was a frequent meeting-place of elves from far and wide.

One day pretty young Janet from the nearby mansion happened to wander into these woods. She picked some bluebells here, some ferns there, until suddenly she came upon a clearing which was filled with rose bushes covered in flowers. She ran up to them and carefully broke off a sprig with three flowers on it. Then her knees gave way beneath her, as she heard from behind her back a voice sterner than any which had ever spoken to her before:

"You, girl: how dare you pick flowers in an elfin forest?"

"Forgive me, I did not know."

"That's what they all say. I am the guardian of this wood, and I watch over it day and night, so that no one may intrude on their property," he said in a quiet voice. He could not take his eyes off the pretty young girl.

"Don't worry, I shan't hurt you," he added in a moment, and he broke off three blossoming sprigs and handed them to her.

"Tell me, who are you, and what is your name?" asked Janet, feeling bolder now. "People say the elves' knights are quite different."

"I am called Tam, and I guard this wood. And what is your name?"

"Janet. I came from yon mansion to spend a while in the woods. Do not punish me, Tam," she begged him, "for I have done nothing evil. I have heard you are the most renowned of the elf-queen's knights."

Tam smiled suddenly.

"Don't you worry; I couldn't harm you if I wanted to. Only

take these roses from me. I am no elf, Janet, but was born here like yourself."

The girl was too surprised to utter a word. Then the young man told her how his parents had died when he was small, and how he had been brought up by his grandfather. When he was twelve years old his grandfather allowed him, after much pleading, to go out with a hunting party. It was a cold morning, and he was suddenly unable to keep pace with the galloping company. No one noticed that he had fallen behind the rest, and he suddenly tumbled from his mount, for his numbed fingers were unable to keep hold of the rein in the biting north wind. When he came back to his senses, he found that he was in the kingdom of the elves. Their queen had carried him off as he lay senseless beneath a tree.

"Since that day I have been enchanted, in the power of the elves. I cannot return among people, and I follow only the elf-queen's orders," Tam added.

Janet wrung her hands; she had never met with any ill in her life before.

"You can surely break the elves' spell and escape from their kingdom; just tell me quickly how!"

"It is hard to overcome elf-magic," sighed the young man, "very hard indeed; and whoever tries and fails can expect no mercy from them. Perish the thought!"

But the girl went on asking, until at last Tam told her:

"Tonight at midnight is the very time when a bold man might indeed escape from the elves. The whole of the queen's company will take horse, and we shall all cross the forest to the deserted castle to welcome the coming of summer. If no one helps me on that journey, I shall stay in the elf-queen's power for another year, and no power on earth can overcome it."

That was just what Janet had wanted to hear; now she only needed to know what she would have to do to set the young man free.

Tam took hold of both her hands.

"You, too, would fare ill, for all men fear the vengeance of [178] the elves. Only someone who is not afraid of anything they threaten, and will not let go of me, can break the queen's power."

"If that is all there is to it," Janet comforted him, "if that is all there is to it, then have no fear. I shall not be afraid of anything in the world. Just tell me what I am to do."

Little by little, Tam told her everything he had learnt among the elves.

"If you really wish to set me free, then wait at midnight at the crossing of the ways, until you hear the elves' horses. At the head of the procession will be the queen of the elves herself with her train; take no notice of them, and make sure you are well hidden from them. Let the second group of riders pass, too, but when the third approaches, pay attention! I shall be riding in it on a horse as white as snow, and you will recognize me by my golden coronet. When I pass you, you must not hesitate even for an instant, or it will be too late. Jump out, catch my horse's rein, quickly pull me out of the saddle, and hold me in your arms, whatever may happen to me. But you must not cry out, or speak a word; otherwise you cannot set me free!"

Long before midnight, Janet was waiting at the crossing of the ways, crouching in the bushes. She was stiff with cold and fright, but she did not move a muscle, lest the rustle of leaves or the crackle of twigs might give her away. It was as if she were growing out of the ground.

Then she heard the quiet sound of horses' hooves in the distance, and soon the silver saddle and bridle of a black horse were shining out of the darkness. Dressed in green silk, the queen of the elves rode along proudly, followed by her train. Janet dared not even breathe lest they caught sight of her. She remained still, too, as the second group of riders passed. Now the third party was on its way, among its number a horse whiter than snow, its rider wearing a golden coronet which gleamed in the moonlight. Janet leapt out from the bushes, took hold of the white horse's rein, pulled the rider swiftly down from the saddle, and held him tightly in her arms.

At that moment there was an angry whispering from all sides, as though a great many drums were all being beaten at once: "Tam! Tam! Tam!"

The queen of the elves turned her horse and galloped up to Janet. She looked the girl up and down with a malevolent eye, and then Janet was almost petrified with fear, as she saw that she was embracing a lizard. Before she had recovered herself, she was holding a snake instead of a lizard, and it very nearly slipped out of her fingers. Janet sank her teeth into her bottom lip; it was high time to stifle a cry, for just then the elf-queen changed the young man into a glowing coal. Tears streamed from the girl's eyes in her pain, and they slowly extinguished the fire.

Now the queen of the elves saw that Janet had defeated her, and had broken her power over Tam. At that instant Tam changed into a handsome young man.

The queen took a last malicious glance at Janet and her loved one. She did them no harm, but only said angrily:

"Well, Tam, off you go with your Janet: you are free as a bird beneath the clouds. If I had thought Janet might enter my woods and carry off the dearest of my knights, I should have whipped her with thorns with my own hands and torn out her hair; I should have turned her into a monster. Well, then, be off with you, and never let me see you again!"

At that the queen spurred on her black horse, taking Tam's white one by the rein, and the riders galloped off as swiftly as they had come. They did not trample a blade of grass or break off a single twig. They were gone like the mist in the morning sun.

After that Janet and Tam lived in happiness and contentment, and would often tell their children and grandchildren of the queen of the elves and her company.

The Princess
from the Enchanted Castle

A long, long time ago, there lived a certain Irish prince. When he reached those years of his life when the wise counsellors of the court were worrying over where to find a suitable wife for him, he set off himself to the distant Eastern Lands, whence he wished to bring a bride. No one knows whether he had seen some beautiful princess already, or if some wise counsellor advised him. But he surely knew why he was setting out on such a journey. He had a long trek before he finally found his princess, and when he did so that was far from being the end of his trials.

The princess lived in a great castle on a tall rock, around which huge wheels turned, night and day. No one could enter the castle while those wheels were turning.

The Irish prince arrived below the castle, walked all round it, examined it from all sides, and then hung his head.

"What good was it coming here?" he sighed, sadly. "Why have I travelled so far, when I am unable to enter the castle and gaze on the beautiful princess?"

He would have turned and gone away, if one of the castle windows had not opened. The prince looked up, and saw the most beautiful creature in the whole world. He had never even dreamed of a woman so lovely. She was the daughter of the King of the Eastern Lands. She lived with her servants in a tower surrounded by ever-turning wheels. The king had had them put there, and set them in motion himself, so that no one might get to his daughter, for he wished her to wed a powerful neighbouring king. But this neighbour was not only rich and powerful, but old and ugly to boot, and the princess did not want him.

The princess gazed sadly at the Irish prince and as their eyes met the young man was rooted to the spot.

After some little time, the prince said, "I shall return to Ireland. But I promise you that I shall not rest, or eat twice at the same table, until I have found the most powerful magician in my country. When I find one skilled enough to halt these huge wheels, I shall come back for you. I beg you to wait until I return."

"Only there is no such magician in Ireland," a voice said suddenly from just beside the prince. From out of nowhere a wizened old man had appeared at his side.

"How should you know? There are many wise old men in Ireland," replied the prince.

"Indeed there are, but I tell you that apart from the King of the Eastern Lands there is only one person in the world who can stop those huge wheels, and he is not in Ireland."

"Then where is he? Who is he?"

"Standing here before you; it is I" said the old man, gravely.

"And who might you be?" asked the prince.

"Does it matter? Once, when I was young, I was a friend of the King of the East. We have not met for many years, but we once studied under the greatest of all wizards. In those days I was always the better magician, and I suppose I might still outdo him and stop the great wheels in front of the castle, if you were to ask me to."

"Halt the wheels, I implore you," the Irish prince replied. "And tell me who you are, to whom I shall be grateful for the rest of my life, and what you ask in return."

"I am the mighty wizard Thuraoi of Ireland, and I ask no more than to be allowed to take from the castle what I like best."

"Thank you for your offer of help, but the castle is not mine," replied the Irish prince.

"A trifle," called the princess from the window. "My dear Thuraoi, if you help us to stop the wheels, so that the prince may enter the castle, you may take what you wish. Everything you like in the castle shall be yours."

"Do you both promise me?" asked the wizard.

"We promise," replied prince and princess with one voice.

Then the mighty magician ordered the prince to retire with him to a distance of nine paces from the huge wheels. As the pair of them took the ninth step and came to a halt, the great wheels were stilled in an instant. The prince ran into the castle, and the princess ran to meet him.

The King of the Eastern Lands was most startled to find that the wheels in front of the castle had stopped and, calling to his guard, he ran with drawn sword to see what intruder had overcome his defences. But when the king caught sight of Thuraoi the magician, the sword fell from his hand, and he knew that there was nothing he could do.

"Why have you come?" he asked in a little while.

"I am an Irish prince, and I have come for your daughter. The mighty Thuraoi helped me, and your daughter and I have promised in return that he may take the thing he likes best from the castle."

"Is it so, my daughter?" the king asked the princess.

"Yes, father," the lovely girl replied, and quickly gave the prince a smile.

"Choose what you want from the castle," said the king, turning to the wizard.

"I have already chosen," replied Thuraoi. "The thing I like best in the whole castle is your daughter. From this moment she is mine."

The king, the princess and the unfortunate Irish prince all gasped. [184]

But there was nothing they could do — a promise was a promise. The princess almost died of grief that she should have to marry the old wizard. Tears streamed from her eyes when she looked at the Irish prince. From that moment on her sorrow was seven times greater. She would far sooner have lain beneath the sod forever than hold out her hand to the crafty wizard.

Luckily, the Irish prince managed to whisper to her that she should not despair, that he would try to deliver her from the magician. The princess cheered up a little, and resolved to put off the wedding as long as possible.

"I have promised to go with you," she told the wizard, "and I shall keep my promise. But I, too, have a request, and ask you to grant it. I want you to take me to your castle immediately after the wedding, and I want that castle to be at least as big and grand as my father's. You surely cannot expect me to live more humbly as your wife than as a maiden?"

"Very well. Soon you shall have a castle such as you desire," the wizard promised the beautiful princess. He would gladly have promised her the moon and the stars, let alone a beautiful castle. "All my men shall cross the whole of Ireland in search of the biggest boulders. Within a year you shall have a castle in Ireland finer than any in the world."

"Go back to Ireland, my dearest," the princess begged the prince. "Go and watch secretly the building of the wizard's castle. Send me a message when it is almost completed, and I shall come with my retinue to see it. I trust we shall find some way to get the better of him."

The Irish prince did as the princess had asked him and, dressed as a wandering minstrel, he watched as mighty giants brought boulders to build the wizard's castle. He saw the high, rough walls grow taller day by day, and observed the cabinet-makers of all Ireland constructing tables and chairs for the castle halls, the blacksmiths forging metal, the goldsmiths beating the most wonderful ornaments, the weavers working day and night, and the women embroidering curtains, carpets and drapes, so that all might be ready as soon as possible, and all of untold beauty.

There was only a month to go before the promised year was up, when the Irish prince secretly sent word to his beloved princess to come and see the new castle, since all was nearly finished.

The princess set out at once for Ireland with a great retinue, and the old wizard jumped for joy like a hot-headed youth. When the ship of the King of the Eastern Lands dropped anchor on the coast of Ireland, it was greeted not only by crowds of curious onlookers, but also by the song of a wandering minstrel. The princess had never heard such a beautiful song, and at once she begged the magician, "My dearest, summon that minstrel to the castle: let him cheer us all with his singing."

During the singing and merrymaking, the princess found time to whisper to the minstrel to bring his finest warriors to the woods beneath the castle, and to wait there by the stream.

"When you see milk flowing in the stream, you will know that our time has come. Quickly bring your men to the castle gates. I shall be waiting for you there."

The prince did as she asked, and soon he and the pick of his men were hidden in the wood below the castle. They watched the stream day and night to see if milk might flow in it instead of water.

Days went by; the castle grew in size, and the wizard's giants were bringing the last of the boulders. Old Thuraoi was waiting impatiently for the workmen to finish the building, so that he might show the princess that there really was no castle more beautiful in the whole wide world. He grew tired of waiting, so at last he set out hunting to while away the time.

This was the moment the princess from the Eastern Lands had been waiting for. That evening when the servants milked the cows, she turned her nose up at the milk.

"Fie! How the milk stinks today!" she said. "Pour it all in the stream! I don't want to see a single drop left in the pails. Who knows what poison there is in it!"

The servant-girls were most surprised, and tried to persuade the princess that the milk was fresh and good. But it was no use: in the end the princess stamped her foot and cried, "Pour the milk in the stream and be done with it, or you will regret it!"

So the servant-girls and footmen carried the full pails of milk down to the stream, for the wizard had given strict orders that the princess was to be obeyed in all things, or it would be the worse for them.

As soon as the stream in the forest turned white with milk, the prince and his company leapt up and ran headlong towards the castle gate. The princess from the Eastern Lands was waiting there with her whole retinue.

"Quickly, quickly," she urged her loved one. "The wizard and his companions are out hunting. Now is the time to escape!"

The prince's faithful warriors overcame the guards, and they all took flight.

Late in the evening the magician returned home to find the castle empty. There was no sign of the guards, nor of his trusty giants, nor of the princess and her courtiers. Beside himself with rage, he ran to the top of the tower, took a huge horn from his back, and blew a loud blast on it to summon help. But the giants with their boulders were still far away, and before they had taken their heavy loads from their backs and run with seven-mile strides to their master, the old wizard had torn himself apart with rage. When the giants ran to the top of the the tower, they found him lying blackened on the ground, and never found out why he had summoned them.

The Irish prince, with his beloved princess and his faithful warriors, arrived home safely, and at once celebrated the greatest of weddings. For nine days they drank ale and mead, and ate the choicest foods; they danced and made merry until all the stones of the wizard's castle rolled down into the valley below. And that took a good long time, so the young couple lived happily and merrily to a ripe old age.

The Youngest Brother

In ancient times there lived a king in whose garden there was a beautiful pear tree. In autumn a single golden pear would ripen on it every night. The pears were the king's dearest treasures, for there were more stones in his lands than fields, more cliffs than trees. Then, one year, some creature came night after night and stole the precious pear. The king set guards on the tree in vain: every morning the pear had disappeared as if it had melted into thin air.

"My son," the king said at last to the eldest of the princes. "To-night you shall guard the pear tree. Take your bow and arrow, and make an end of the thief who is bringing about our downfall."

So the eldest prince went into the garden with his companions. The young men sat down in the grass around the tree, leant their bows against their knees, prepared their arrows, and then laid out tasty meat and white bread, which they washed down with wine as golden as a ripe pear from the magic tree. Morning was still far off when the prince and his company fell into a deep sleep. The young men did not hear the wind bending the crowns of the trees, nor the waves of the sea pounding against the rocks. They were lost to the world, until the morning sun began to stroke them. Then they leapt to their feet, looked at the tree, and froze with horror. The golden pear was gone without trace, as if it had never been there at all.

The king flew into such a rage that sparks flew from his eyes.

"My son," he said to the middle of the three princes, "show that you are more able than your brother. Take your sword, bow and arrows, and save the pear from this thief!"

So the middle brother took his turn at guarding the tree with his companions. The young men feasted until they slept like logs. In the morning the leaves of the tree were as green as in springtime, but there was no sign of the golden fruit.

There was a great to-do in the castle when the king heard what had happened.

"My son," he said to the youngest prince, at last. "Woe betide you if you do not save the pear from the thief. Do not show your face without it!"

The youngest prince took his bow and arrows, and as evening fell he went into the garden alone, without companions.

The night seemed long, as he stared into the darkness, with no sound or light to relieve it. Not a leaf stirred, even the distant sea forgot to roar. It was almost dawn before a huge eagle descended silently from the clouds, dropped on the pear like a stone, took the fruit in its beak, and flew out of the tree like lightning. At that moment the prince shot his arrow: the bird gave a screech that made the trees in the garden quiver and the sea cliffs ring. The golden pear fell from its beak, and the eagle flew off, slowly and with difficulty. The youngest prince ran to where he could see a gleam in the dark, and found the golden pear at the bottom of the garden. He returned to the castle, and his father was waiting for him.

"Well, my son, did you save the golden pear?"

"Here it is, father. A great eagle carried it off, but my arrow surely struck it, for it gave a loud cry and flew away, letting the pear drop from its beak."

The king had the two elder brothers awoken at once, and began to scold them: "You two did not save the most precious of the royal treasures, for revelling, wine and sleep were dearer to you. Therefore neither of you shall succeed to the throne. Only your younger brother deserves the crown."

When they heard these words, the two brothers went away with their heads hung low, and plotted a wicked revenge on their brother; he, however, had no notion of it.

"Come with me, brothers," he called to them in a while. "Let us go into the garden. Perhaps I really killed the thieving eagle, and we may find it lying somewhere."

The elder brothers trudged after him towards the pear tree.

"Here are some drops of blood in the grass — this is where I hit him!" the youngest prince called suddenly, and they followed the trail of blood a good distance, until they came to an old, half caved-in well. There the trail ended, as if the eagle had fallen in.

"Now we shall see!" said the eldest brother, suddenly getting an idea. "Let me down into the well on the rope, but pull me up at once if I tug on it."

Slowly, little by little, they let the eldest prince down. But he had not got far when he gave a tug on the rope. They hauled him up quickly, and he gasped:

"I tell you, my lads, it's as dark as a dungeon in there, and there's a stink fit to choke you, as though the shaft led down to hell itself! I thought you would not pull me out alive!"

The middle brother was not to be put off, and he, too, had himself let down into the well. But before long he tugged on the rope, and when his brothers hauled him out, he could scarcely stand. The two elder brothers would have gone away, but the youngest held them back.

"Wait a moment," he told them. "I shall take a look. Perhaps I shall discover something after all."

So they let the youngest down, slowly, bit by bit, so that they should not have far to haul him back. But the prince did not tug on the string, did not ask to be pulled out. For a long time he saw nothing in the blackness, and he was about ready to go up again, when he suddenly saw a light far below him. Now he went down more boldly, and just as his brothers at the top of the well came to the end of the rope, he found himself standing on the bottom. It was quite dry, and in front of him an underground world opened out. He looked around boldly, and saw that all was as neat and pretty as in his father's garden. He ran across a flowering meadow, and the path led him into a wood. He started as he suddenly saw a bent old woman.

"Good day, old woman," the prince greeted her.

"Good day to you, prince. What are you doing here?"

"I am seeking the thief who stole the golden pears. Last night I shot him, as he was taking the last pear from the tree. I know that he went into the well, but he is not there."

"There is no need to look further; he is here. And he is my son, a powerful wizard. You are helpless against him — your efforts are in vain. I have just come from him, from the steel castle on the other side of the forest. Mark my words: leave him alone and return home, or you will regret it!"

The prince thanked her for her advice, but he did not return. He strode briskly towards the steel castle beyond the forest. As he stepped out of the thicket, the castle gleamed in front of him like a bright sword. On a tall pillar in front of the gate an eagle was sitting, its wings folded and its head beneath its feathers. The moment it saw the young man, it gave an ear-piercing shriek, spread its wings, and flew off heavily, more like a wounded bird than a mighty king.

At the sound of the eagle's cry, a young girl came out of the castle. She was so beautiful that the prince thought he might be dreaming.

She stood stock still when she caught sight of him in front of the gate.

"Welcome, stranger!" she said, when she had recovered herself. "How pleased I am to see a human face again after so long. Come inside, sit down and rest, and tell me how you got here. Do not be afraid — the eagle will not return so quickly."

"I have not come to sit or rest, and I am not afraid of the eagle. I came here after him, for he stole a golden pear from my father's tree every night. He was sitting on the pillar here a moment ago."

"From your father he stole pears, but from my father, the King of Spain, he took his only joy — his three daughters. He has imprisoned us all here — the eldest in a golden castle, the middle one in a silver castle, and me, the youngest, in this steel castle."

"And do you know how I can deliver you from this underground world?" the prince asked.

"I do. But it is no easy matter, for the eagle is a powerful wizard. It is necessary to pierce him through with his own sword, in which his magic powers lie. But I do not know where the sword is hidden. I only know it is not here in the steel castle."

"Very well," replied the prince, "I shall go in search of the sword. Just tell me the way to your elder sister."

The beautiful princess first fed the youngest prince well, then she set off with him to find her middle sister. But as they were leaving the castle, she handed him a steel slipper.

"May it bring you good fortune in battle!" she told him, and the prince hid the slipper away.

As they drew near the silver castle, they suddenly heard the eagle shriek fit to burst their eardrums; it circled over them, and flew away painfully.

Words cannot tell how glad the middle princess was to see her sister and the prince. But when they mentioned the eagle's sword, she sighed, "I know the eagle's sword, but he never leaves it here."

"If that is so, then we shall be on our way again; perhaps your eldest sister knows something of the sword," said the youngest prince.

The prince and princesses set off quickly for the golden castle. As they left, the second princess gave the prince a silver slipper. "May it bring you good fortune in battle!" she told him, and he hid it away.

The gleam of the golden castle could be seen from afar; it was as though flames were leaping from it, and that was only the reflection of the sun on its golden walls and towers.

Suddenly, the eagle gave a terrible shriek from the tallest tower, nearly deafening the three travellers. Then it spread its wings and flew off.

What rejoicing there was when the sisters embraced, and the eldest welcomed the prince to the golden castle! The princess would gladly have given him anything in the world, but the prince wanted only the magic sword.

"If that is all, then I will gladly bring it to you, for I know where the eagle has it hidden in the tower. But first take this golden slipper, and may it bring you good fortune in battle."

When the prince had hidden the slipper, the girl hurried off, and returned as swiftly as the wind. She was holding in both hands a great sword, so heavy she could scarcely lift it. The blade was of steel, the hilt of gold and silver, set with precious stones, with a mighty eagle's head staring out from it.

"Wait in front of the castle for the eagle," the princess told the youngest prince, "and when he is about to pounce on you, thrust the point of the sword at him. When you stab him, he will turn into a man, as helpless as a child. He will return to his mother, and from that moment we shall be free, and can return with you to the world above. But take care, for the eagle has great strength, even though you have wounded him."

Before the eldest sister had had time to say all she wished to, they saw the eagle approaching. It flew like the wind, soared high in the air, then dropped like a stone on the prince. The young man stepped aside, as pliant as a willow wand, and raised the sword. As the eagle was pierced by its point, it let out a shriek that might almost have cracked open the castle's golden walls — and all its magic powers were gone. It changed into a feeble old man, as tattered as a beggar. He scowled at the young man with the sword in his hand, and at the eldest daughter of the King of Spain, then shuffled off into the forest without turning his head again.

Now there was no end to the rejoicing and embracing. But then the sisters' thoughts turned to home, and they wanted to return to their father without delay. They suddenly became grave.

"How are we to get back to the kingdom of Spain, when we do not know the way?" cried the eldest. "There is no one to tell us, no one to help us."

"Have no fear," said the prince. "Just come along with me with a bold heart. I know the way to the well in our garden, and my brothers are waiting there. They will pull us all out, and then we shall send you with all speed to the kingdom of Spain."

The journey back passed quickly. When they got to the well-shaft, the youngest brother tugged on the rope for his brothers to haul him up. Then he tied the eldest sister to the rope, then the middle one, and finally the youngest.

The two elder brothers almost swooned with amazement when they pulled the girls out of the well — each more beautiful than the next — and heard how their youngest brother had set them free. At first they rejoiced with all their hearts to see the princesses. But then they were seized with envy, and when only their brother was waiting to be hauled up, they threw the rope down into the well.

"Wait a while, until someone comes to get you out, dear brother!" called the eldest. And the middle brother added:

"If you are such a hero and king-to-be, then maybe you can climb up without our help, or fly out like the eagle!"

The frightened girls had to swear that they would tell no one who had set them free, or what the elder brothers had done. Then the two princes took them to a ship, set sail, and made for the kingdom of Spain.

The king was as pleased as a little child to see his daughters, whom he had long since given up for lost, alive and well. Straight away he had the city hung with red and decorated with flowers, and did not know how to thank the two deceitful princes.

Meanwhile, the youngest brother wandered, lost, about the underworld. When he could find no way home, he looked for the castles from which he had freed the princesses. But it was as if the earth had swallowed them up: there was not a trace of them. In the end he met the wizard's mother.

"Now you see, prince, that evil has indeed befallen you, since you would not leave my son alone, as I warned you. You have brought evil days upon him; he is weak and helpless since he was wounded with his own sword. But you are also weak and helpless, though his sword hangs at your side. Return it to him, and he will take you up to the royal garden, and never venture into your father's kingdom again."

The youngest prince agreed, and the moment the magician took his sword in his hands he changed into a mighty eagle again.

"Quickly, prince, sit on my back; I shall take you straight to the kingdom of Spain, where the princess is waiting for you, and nearly crying her eyes out on your account."

Early in the morning the eagle alighted on a cliff overlooking the royal city, and took his leave of the prince. The young man made his way into the city by the shortest route. When he got there, all was spick and span, and the bells were ringing as if to welcome him.

"What is happening?" the prince asked, at the nearest tavern.

The taverner saw a tired and tattered lad, and replied carelessly.

"As every child in the country knows, the two elder princesses are marrying their deliverers, and the king is looking for a husband for the youngest. There would be suitors enough, but she will have only the one who brings her a steel slipper."

"There is nothing simpler than to grant the princess's wish," smiled the young man. "Take these three slippers; first give the golden one to the eldest princess, then the silver one to the middle princess, and then give the youngest the steel slipper she asks. You may ask what you will of the grooms for the first two slippers, but do not ask the youngest princess for anything."

When the taverner arrived at the royal castle, the sentries did not want to let him in, but when he showed them that he was taking rare slippers to the princesses, they finally led him to the royal hall. When the two elder princesses saw their slippers, they at once gave orders for the taverner to be given a purse of gold and a purse of silver. But the youngest princess gave orders for the servants to harness the fastest horses to her carriage.

Soon she and the taverner arrived at the tavern on the edge of the city, looking for the ragged fellow who had sent her the steel slipper.

The bridegrooms saw that the game was up, slipped out of the royal hall, and took to their heels. But in vain: when the king heard the truth, he fumed with rage, and sent his fastest riders after the pair. They found them and brought them back to the king in chains. The youngest princess had already returned with her beloved prince.

The two elder brothers flung themselves on their knees before the king and their younger brother, and begged forgiveness for what they had done when envy had turned their heads.

"To the dungeons with them!" cried the king.

But the youngest prince and princess pleaded for them, and in the end the king said, "If your brother has forgiven the wrong you did him, then I shall pardon you."

The three brothers shook hands and embraced, and at that moment all ills were forgotten. They quickly sent for their father to come to the royal wedding, and then there was great merrymaking. It did not even end in a year and a day, for then the pears ripened in the royal garden again and the king gave one to each of his grandchildren, and he and the Spanish king had cause to celebrate all over again.

What the Storyteller Did
when He Ran out of Stories

Long ago in the kingdom of Leinster, the king had a very fine story-teller. Every evening he would send for him, and the storyteller would always tell him a new tale. He had been telling him stories every evening for twice seven years, and had never told the same one twice. He always had a new tale at his fingertips. The king set great store by his storyteller; he had a fine house built for him beside the palace, and made him presents of royal horses and noble dogs, but sometimes he would vent his anger on him of an evening.

Before the storyteller had even opened his mouth, the king would cry, "Get on with it! I know it! I've heard it all before. Tell me a new story, or I'll have you banished in disgrace, or even worse."

Once the storyteller had the courage to say to the king, "Forgive me, my liege, but sometimes one can be helpless, unable to put one's thoughts together or to decide what to do. And in such a moment of weakness, which all of us have, would you really have me banished in disgrace, when I have served you faithfully for twice seven years? Or punish me even more severely?"

The king grew red with anger:

"Never speak to me like that again!" he shouted. "I am not helpless, and I never will be! The King of Leinster is powerful, and his will shall always be done. I should rather die than be helpless!"

The storyteller hung his head silently, and tried to please the king, but he was not able to tell his tales as well as he should have done, for he was afraid of the king's wrath.

In the end the storyteller always managed to think up a story which made the king forget his troubles and worries, and then he would sleep tight until dawn. The king would not have parted with his storyteller for half a kingdom, but he never let it be known.

Every morning the storyteller would go out into the garden, and as he walked up and down he would make up the next evening's tale. But one day he just could not think of one. As soon as he had thought of *Once upon a time there were three Irish princes,* that was as far as he got. Then he started another type: *Once upon a time there was an old beggar* — but he could think of nothing the beggar might do that the king had not already heard. He wished the ground would swallow him up in his shame. His wife called him to table, but he snapped back at her, "Until I have thought up this evening's story, I will not eat!"

"Very well, but tell me what that black thing on the hill overlooking the garden is," his wife replied.

"I don't know, I have never seen any black thing there," said the storyteller, gruffly.

"Then let us go and take a look — maybe you will think of something on the way."

So the storyteller whistled to his favourite dog, and they went to see what the dark shape on the hill was. When they got there, they found a tattered old beggar with a wooden leg. He was sitting on a bank, shaking some dice in a heavy wooden cup.

"Who are you, and what do you want here?"

"Can't you see that I am a tattered old beggar with a wooden leg?" retorted the old man. "I am taking a rest, and waiting for someone to play dice with me, so that I may forget the pain and the grief for a while at least."

"And do you suppose anyone will play dice with you?"

"Why not?" replied the beggar. "I have a purse with exactly a hundred sovereigns. For such riches it is worth playing even with an old beggar."

"Play with him," the storyteller's wife whispered to her husband. "I expect you will have a story for the king when you are done."

The storyteller sat down on the bank beside the beggar. There was a big stone there, as flat as a table, so they began to play right away. The storyteller kept losing. Soon he had nothing left: not a copper in the house, nor even a house, nor a carriage, nor horses, nor dogs. Any beggar was richer than he.

"Well, now I have a tale for the king!" he burst out angrily. "Then he will have me banished at once in ridicule!"

"Play on — you may yet win. Fortune must smile on you once at least," his wife encouraged him.

"But you know well enough that I am worse off than the poorest beggar — I haven't even a beggar's stick!"

"You still have a wife. Let us play for her!" the beggar urged him.

Well, believe it or not, they played for his wife, and the storyteller lost yet again. The beggar sat down beside her at once, smiled at her pleasantly, and said, "Have no fear, we shall be happy together. I shall just play one more game with the king's storyteller."

"But you have taken everything: what else could you want?" asked the storyteller.

"You. We shall play for you. If you win, all that you have lost shall be yours again, and my sovereigns to boot. If you lose, then you are mine, too," the beggar persuaded him.

In a while the storyteller, too, belonged to the beggar.

"Very well," said the beggar, satisfied. "Now you are mine also. Now tell me what animal I am to change you into — a hare, a deer, a fox? Maybe a wild boar?"

"Does it matter?" cried the storyteller. "A hare is as good as anything."

The beggar struck the storyteller with a magic wand, and in a flash a hare was hopping about on the bank. Before he had properly twitched his ears, the storyteller's dog was after him. It chased him around the gorse bushes, and up and down the furrows, and finally caught him by the neck and took him alive to the beggar.

"Good dog, good dog!" The beggar patted the animal. Then he struck the storyteller with his wand once more, and the hare became a man again. He could scarcely catch his breath for terror.

"It were better you had let the dog tear me apart!" he cried in despair.

"Why? Until now you never knew how a poor hare feels when the hunting dogs chase him. Now you know, and you can tell the king," replied the beggar.

"And will you not tell me who you are, and why you are playing with me like a cat with a mouse?"

"If you really want to know, come along with me," offered the beggar. "I promise that by evening you will have seen many things, and will be wiser than you were before."

"Very well," the storyteller agreed.

The beggar whistled, and in a flash there was a well-dressed old man with a long white beard standing beside him.

"Take care of this woman, and her house, carriage, horses and dogs," the beggar ordered him. "Keep them from all danger, and bring them to us when I call."

Then the beggar caught the storyteller's sleeve, and at that moment they both became invisible, though they could see all that went on around them. They set off, and both entered the royal castle, quite unseen. The king had just eaten and drunk his fill, and now all he needed was a good story.

"Go and fetch my storyteller!" he ordered the servants.

Soon the servants returned with the news that the storyteller's house was empty, that not even a dog barked there, and that there was neither sight nor sound of the storyteller or his wife.

"He shall pay dearly for this!" shouted the king.

Then the beggar whispered quietly to the storyteller, "Wait a moment; my time has come!" He leaned on the door, and at that instant again became a tattered beggar, thin and wearing worn-out shoes.

"What are you doing here?" a guard asked fiercely.

"I have come to entertain the king. I am returning from far away, from the deep valleys where the white swans sing. I spent one night on an island, the next on the mainland. I saw many things, experienced many things; perhaps the king would like to hear of them."

"I shall listen when the harpists have finished their playing," replied the king. "All the best harpists from all five parts of Ireland are assembled in my court. They came from the north and the south, the east and the west and the middle to play for me. Tell me, have you ever heard more lovely music?" he asked the ragged beggar.

"Indeed I have. I do not say that they play badly, but compared to the harpists I heard not long ago on the Isle of Man, their playing is like a cat purring by the fireside, or like mosquitoes buzzing around a lamp, or like an angry old woman quarrelling with her husband."

When the royal harpists heard this, they put aside their harps, drew their swords, and threw themselves upon the beggar. But so blinded were they by their anger that they did not harm a hair of his head, for they chopped and cut each other instead.

"Enough!" roared the king. "Is it not enough that my storyteller has gone off somewhere, and that I shall have no story today — am I to have no peace either? Hang this ragamuffin!"

The guards leapt upon the beggar and dragged him into the courtyard, out of the gate, and over to the scaffold. They did not even ask what his last wish might be. Then they returned to the royal hall, satisfied with their work, and who should they see there sitting on a bench drinking ale and eating roast mutton, but the skinny old beggar?

"Didn't we just hang you? How did you get back into the royal hall?" the captain of the guard yelled at him.

"Take a good look at me," said the beggar, quietly. "How can you have hanged me, when you see with your own eyes how the king's ale is to my liking?" And he took a swig from the big mug.

The guards ran outside the gate to take a look. When they returned from the gallows, their hair was standing on end and their eyes popping out of their heads. They called the captain to one side, and quietly whispered in his ear, so that the king would not hear:

"The king's three younger brothers are swinging on the scaffold. If the king finds out, it will be the end of us!"

At that moment the king glanced at the table, and saw that the beggar was still sitting there drinking ale.

"Guards, did I not tell you to hang that scoundrel? Is this how you obey my orders? I shall have you hanged as well, and that will be the end of that!"

"Mercy!" cried the guards, throwing themselves on their knees before the king. "We did hang the scoundrel, but there was some sort of mishap. When we saw him in here, we went to look outside, and we saw your brothers swinging there."

Quite beside himself, the king rushed out to the scaffold to see for himself. There was no sign of his brothers, but in their place hung all the king's harpists, harps and all.

Half the guards fled in terror, and the king stood as if rooted to the ground; but the captain of the guard at least had the courage to grab hold of the beggar and drag him off to the scaffold again.

"How many more times will you send me into the next world?" the beggar asked. "And all because I did not like the king's music."

"And what of the king's brothers, and the harpists?" demanded the captain of the guard.

"Just take a good look; see how they are sitting contentedly in the shade in front of the gate, enjoying their ale!"

All who were present turned to look, and indeed, the king's brothers and the harpists were sitting on the grass in the evening breeze, and it was clear that the ale was to their taste. The king's knees were so wobbly with amazement when he saw that it really was them, that he could scarcely manage to make his way over to them to refresh himself with them.

The beggar suddenly disappeared as if he had never been at the king's court at all. He ran back with the storyteller to the bank where they had played dice that morning, and the storyteller's wife, horses, carriage and dogs were waiting there.

"Quickly, take all that belongs to you and return to the royal court," the beggar said. "Now you have a good tale for the king."

The storyteller shook his head.

"I lost everything," he sighed.

"You lost nothing," the beggar told him, "for I did not play fairly, but with the help of magic. As you can see, it was good magic. So that you may know, I am no ordinary fellow, but Angus the magician, and I know how well you have served the King of Leinster. That is why I wished to help you, when I saw how troubled you were this morning."

But the storyteller still did not move.

"You may go," the beggar continued. "You and your wife are free. I shall not bother you any more. Instead I shall listen to your stories from time to time in the royal castle, for there is nothing to beat a good storyteller. I knew how to change you into a hare and have the dog catch you, but no one can catch your stories; they fly free through the whole kingdom."

The storyteller wanted to thank him, but the beggar was gone. So he went straight to the king and told him the whole story down to the last detail.

"When you have no more stories to tell," the king said to him at last, when the storyteller fell silent, "then just tell me this one again. We shall have a good laugh at it. And if I should forget how helpless and faint-hearted I was before that beggar, just tell it to me over again; from such a fine storyteller as yourself it will always be dear to me."